CONTENTS

The New Books Kids Like

EDITED BY
Sharon Deeds
Catherine Chastain

PREPARED FOR
Association for Library Service to Children

AMERICAN LIBRARY ASSOCIATION
Chicago and London
2001

While extensive effort has gone into ensuring the reliability of information appearing in this book, the publisher makes no warranty, express or implied, on the accuracy or reliability of the information, and does not assume and hereby disclaims any liability to any person for any loss or damage caused by errors or omissions in this publication.

Project editor: Louise D. Howe

Cover design: Tessing Design

Composition: ALA Editions in Minion and Friz Quadrata typefaces using QuarkXpress 4.1 for the PC

Printed on 50-pound white offset, a pH-neutral stock, and bound in 10-point cover stock by Batson Printing

The paper used in this publication meets the minimum requirements of American National Standard for Information Sciences—Permanence of Paper for Printed Library Materials, ANSI Z39.48-1992.♾

Library of Congress Cataloging-in-Publication Data

The new books kids like / edited by Sharon Deeds and Catherine Chastain for
    Association for Library Service to Children
       p. cm.
    Includes index.
    ISBN 0-8389-3512-5
    1. Children—Books and reading—United States—Bibliography. 2. Children's
    literature—Bibliography. I. Deeds, Sharon. II. Chastain, Catherine.
    III. Association for Library Service to Children.

Z1037 .N39 2001
011.62—dc21
                                       2001018850

Printed in the United States of America.

05   04   03   02   5   4   3   2

PREFACE

A day doesn't go by when a child, parent, or teacher doesn't ask for assistance in choosing books—good books. With a little bit of questioning, we can usually figure out what a person really wants. Many good sources, both in print and online, index children's books. This book, however, is formatted in the way children ask their questions, such as "Do you have any books about sports?"

In order to compile this annotated bibliography, we sent questionnaires to ALSC members across the country asking them to recommend topics and titles that they have found to be popular with children in kindergarten through fifth grade. A call for input was also sent electronically via PUBYAC and the ALSC electronic discussion lists. Request for input was also featured in the ALSC newsletter. Inclusion was based on quality and on the number of times specific topics and titles were recommended, giving special consideration to titles published since 1991 and still in print. Additions to the lists were made, books were read, annotations were written, and the book began to take shape.

These titles are only the beginning of the discovery of good books. We hope that one good book will lead young readers to another and then another. Children are curious readers. As they learn and grow and become their own beings, their reading tastes expand and run the gamut from dinosaurs to sports to fantasy. They read to be informed, they read because they have to, and they read because it's fun. To hear a child say "Wow, that was a great book. Do you have any more like it?" is music to a librarian's ears. We hope this book will be a helpful resource for children, librarians, and teachers in finding the books that will entice, encourage, and sustain the love of reading.

SHARON DEEDS

CATHERINE CHASTAIN

ACKNOWLEDGMENTS

We extend special thanks to our three contributors, who read many of the suggested books and helped us write the annotations:

Julie Darnall, Chester County (Pennsylvania) Public Library System

Patricia Dollisch, DeKalb County (Georgia) Public Library

Kelly Posey, Forsyth County (Georgia) Public Library

We also thank the librarians listed below, who sent us often-heard questions and recommended books to be included. Without your input this book never could have been written.

Sandra Downs, Barberton Public Library, Barberton, Ohio

Catherine Quattlebaum, Bartram Trail Regional Library, Washington, Georgia

Hedy Harrison, Cerritos Public Library, Cerritos, California

Betty Olszewski, Kathy Stensing, Kathleen Mitchell, and Susan Bender, Dundee Township Library, Dundee, Illinois

Robin Bryant, Eagle Valley Library District, Eagle, Colorado

Carol K. Phillips and Staff, East Brunswick Public Library, East Brunswick, New Jersey

Laurie St. Laurent, East Lansing Public Library, East Lansing, Michigan

Elizabeth Draper, Euless Public Library, Euless, Texas

Marleen Watling, Flower Mound Public Library, Flower Mound, Texas

Carol Kieda, Green Tree Library, Pittsburgh, Pennsylvania

Youth Services Staff of Lindenhurst Memorial Library, Lindenhurst, New York

Mary Ann Nieglos, Little Ferry Free Library, Little Ferry, New Jersey

Susan Quinn, Mifflin County Library, Lewiston, Pennsylvania

Terry Wanser, Norfolk Public Library, Norfolk, Virginia

Denna Wright, Park City Library, Park City, Utah

Zigrida Eberhardt, Reading Public Library, Reading, Pennsylvania

Terry Checkon, Sacramento Public Library, Sacramento, California

Jeane Rinker, Southern Pines Public Library, Southern Pines, North Carolina

Julie Lindsey, Southwest Public Libraries, Grove City, Ohio

Youth Services Staff and Krys Kobertsy, Sterling Heights Public Library, Sterling Heights, Michigan

Merryl Traub, Syosset Public Library, Syosset, New York

Julie Albright, Ventura County Library, Ojai Branch, Ojai, California

Sandra Cope, Waukesha County Library, Waukesha, Wisconsin

Heather Young, Wellesley Free Library, Wellesley, Massachusetts

1

Where Are Your Funny Books?
(Picture Books and Beginning Readers)

Bravo, Amelia Bedelia by Herman Parish
Illustrated by Lynn Sweat   Greenwillow, 1997   GRADES K–2

Amelia Bedelia is back. Once again, Amelia Bedelia takes things literally in a new story written by the nephew of Peggy Parish. Amelia Bedelia is instructed to pick up the "conductor" at the train station. Unfortunately, she returns with the wrong conductor, thus setting off an avalanche of hilarity.

Chato's Kitchen by Gary Soto
Illustrated by Susan Guevara   Putnam, 1995   GRADES K–3

When a family of mice move in next door to a cool cat named Chato, they think he and his good friend Novio Boy are just being nice when they invite them to dinner. They have no idea that the cats are planning to serve them as the main course! This funny cat-and-mouse tale ends with a surprise twist when the mice invite their dachshund friend, Chorizo, to accompany them to dinner.

Cow Buzzed by Andrea Zimmerman
Illustrated by Paul Meisel   Demco, 1995   GRADES K–3

Oh dear, the cow has a cold! But wait, instead of mooing, the cow is buzzing. Now all the farmyard animals have colds and one another's voices and everyone is coughing and sniffling and sneezing—achoo! Tempers flare as the animals blame one another for their colds. Eventually, everything does get back to normal in this funny, participatory tale of mixed-up voices.

Cyrano the Bear by Nicole Rubel
Dial, 1995   GRADES K–3

Mushy but funny story of Cyrano, the bravest sheriff in the West. Unfortunately, he also has the biggest nose in the West and he's sure that the beautiful Roxanne cares little for him. When he's not tracking down the Gila Monster Gang, Cyrano is writing secret love poems to Roxanne. Find out how Cyrano captures the gang and Roxanne's heart!

Dog Breath! The Horrible Trouble with Hally Tosis by Dav Pilkey
Scholastic, 1994   GRADES K–3

Poor Hally, the family dog, has terrible breath! This funny and witty story has the Tosis family looking for cures, such as breathtaking sights, for poor Hally's condition. However, when Hally captures a robber (one lick and down he goes), the Tosis family gladly resorts to, what else, clothespins.

Fox Outfoxed by James Marshall
Dial, 1992   GRADES K–2

Sly, clever fox is outfoxed by his own sister, Louise, and his cute neighbor in three funny tales.

Hat for Minerva Louise by Janet Stoeke
Dutton, 1994   GRADES K–2

Minerva Louise is a naïve hen who looks everywhere for a hat. Kids will love Minerva's funny attempts to find a hat and the inventive solution that keeps her warm.

Hog-Eye by Susan Meddaugh
Houghton Mifflin, 1995   GRADES K–3

A little pig humorously recounts her adventures of getting on the wrong school bus and being captured by a wolf. After realizing that the wolf can't read, she wins her freedom by first outwitting him, then tricking him into believing she has a magic potion—*hog-eye.*

Iktomi and the Buzzard by Paul Goble
Orchard, 1994   GRADES 1–3

One in a series of stories about the misadventures of the Lakota trickster hero. Here sly Iktomi talks a buzzard into giving him a ride on his back, only to be dumped off suddenly when the buzzard notices Iktomi is making rude gestures behind his back. After landing upside-down inside a hollow tree, Iktomi must once again sweet-talk an unsuspecting stranger into helping him out. In addition to the humor inherent in the unusual situations Iktomi gets himself into, Goble adds lots of fun with Iktomi's constant snide asides to the reader.

Julius by Angela Johnson   Illustrated by Dav Pilkey
Orchard, 1993   GRADES K–2

Maya has always wanted a horse or a big brother but when her grandfather sends her a pet pig named Julius, he turns out to be just as much fun. Unfortunately, Julius has some bad habits. He leaves crumbs everywhere, plays loud music, and eats peanut butter right out of the jar. To help him fit in, Maya decides to teach him some manners.

A Million Fish . . . More or Less by Patricia McKissack
Illustrated by Dean Schutzer   Knopf, 1992   GRADES 1–3

Following in the footsteps of local tall-tale tellers Papa-Daddy and Elder Abbajon, young Hugh Thomas claims to have caught a million fish in one day. He then recounts a whopper of a tale about how he lost them all on the way home to a band of raccoon pirates, a flock of crows, and the neighbor's cat.

My Little Sister Ate One Hare by Bill Grossman
Illustrated by Kevin Hawkes   Crown, 1996   GRADES K–2

Not only did she eat a hare, but among other things, snakes, ants, bats, and mice! And she didn't throw up! Except, of course, when she ate ten peas.

Officer Buckle and Gloria by Peggy Rathmann
Putnam, 1995   GRADES K–3

Poor Officer Buckle; no one listens to his school presentations on safety. When Gloria, a police dog, becomes his partner, Officer . . . err . . . Gloria is a big hit. Then one day their presentation is videotaped and Officer Buckle discovers what is really going on. Will jealousy separate the two buddies? A 1996 Caldecott winner.

Pete's a Pizza by William Steig
HarperCollins, 1998   GRADES K–2

Pete's in a bad mood because it's raining outside and he wanted to play ball with his friends. So his father decides to make Pete into a pizza. First

Pete is placed on the table and kneaded like dough. He is tossed and floured and baked and tickled and chased. Then the sun comes out and Pete goes out to play.

Three Stories You Can Read to Your Dog by Sara Swan Miller
Illustrated by True Kelley   Houghton Mifflin, 1997   GRADES K–3

Stories to read to your dog? Yes! This beginning reader is meant to entertain your dog. Children will enjoy the silly dog and his adventures with the burglar, the bone, and the wild dog.

2

Where Are Your
Funny Chapter Books?

Adventures of Captain Underpants by Dav Pilkey
Scholastic, 1997   GRADES 3–5

> Guess what happens when two mischievous boys hypnotize their mean principal? He turns into Captain Underpants, of course. Silliness expands to great waists as Harold and George devise a plan to put mean Mr. Krupp in his place.

Attaboy Sam by Lois Lowry
Illustrated by Diane De Groat   Houghton Mifflin, 1992   GRADES 3–5

> Sam's mother is having a birthday and it's just a few days away. She wants a homemade gift, so Sam decides to make homemade perfume. What are his mother's favorite scents? Newborn babies and homemade bread and chicken soup and just-washed hair. Sam puts all of these ingredients and more into a jar with "smelly" results.

Faith and the Electric Dogs by Patrick Jennings
Scholastic, 1996   GRADES 3–6

> Whoever heard of a talking dog? And not just any talking dog, but a dog who speaks and understands several languages, including Spanish, English, Nahautl, and Cat. When ten-year-old Faith meets such a dog on the streets of Mexico City, strange and interesting things lie ahead for both of them.

Frindle by Andrew Clements
Illustrated by Brian Selznick   Simon & Schuster, 1996   GRADES 3–5

> Nicholas Allen is a smart kid with great ideas. Has he gone too far when he invents a new word for pen. . . *frindle*? Nicholas meets his match in his

dictionary-loving teacher, Mrs. Granger, in this funny, sweet story of his determination to write with a frindle.

Junie B. Jones and the Stupid Smelly Bus by Barbara Park
Illustrated by Denise Brunkus   Random, 1992   GRADES 1–3

It's the first day of kindergarten and Junie B. Jones has to ride the stupid smelly bus. Her first bus ride is a disaster. There's no glove compartment to hold tissues, so you can't even blow your nose! Once settled in school, Junie B. can't face another trip on the bus even if it takes her home. So she hides in a cabinet, and a humorous disaster results.

Later, Gator by Laurence Yep
Hyperion, 1995   GRADES 4–6

Teddy tries to get even with his goody-two-shoes younger brother, Bobby, by buying him a baby alligator for his birthday. But Teddy's prank backfires when Bobby is delighted with his new pet, even though it makes all sorts of trouble in their household. The same two brothers, living in San Francisco's Chinatown, are also featured in *Cockroach Cooties* (Hyperion, 2000).

The Pool Party by Gary Soto
Illustrated by Robert Cesilla   Delacorte, 1993   GRADES 4–6

When Tiffany Perez, the richest kid in school, invites Rudy Herrera to her backyard pool party, Rudy gets all sort of advice and help from his extended family to help him prepare for the event.

Ramona's World by Beverly Cleary
Illustrated by Alan Tiegreen   Morrow, 1999   GRADES 3–5

Ramona's back and she's starting the fourth grade. Beverly Cleary continues the escapades of Ramona and her family with a new addition to the household, a little sister named Roberta. Ramona, now the middle child, is determined to prove her importance in life as she makes new friends, baby-sits for the first time, and has her first crush on a boy she affectionately calls "yard ape."

Rats on the Roof and Other Stories by James Marshall
Dial, 1991   GRADES 1–3

Containing seven silly stories by James Marshall, this short chapter book is perfect for children who have graduated from beginning readers.

Squids Will Be Squids by Jon Scieszka
Illustrated by Lane Smith   Viking, 1998   GRADES 3–5

Morals à la Scieszka anyone? According to the author, "This book . . . is a collection of fables that Aesop might have told if he were alive today and sitting in the back of class daydreaming and goofing around . . . " So tweak your funny bone and get ready to laugh out loud!

Toilet Paper Tigers by Gordon Korman
Scholastic, 1993   GRADES 4–6

It's bad enough that they are coached by a girl. What's worse is that their team uniforms have a picture of toilet paper on the front. Corey's coach, Professor Pendergast, knows nothing about baseball. So the coach's granddaughter Kristy decides to take over the team. And take over she does. Kristy has the entire baseball team wrapped around her little finger after she takes a picture of them in the locker room. When anyone disagrees with her, Kristy threatens to reveal the picture. A humorous story of how one girl is able to turn around a losing baseball team and make them winners.

Wayside School Gets a Little Stranger by Louis Sachar
Illustrated by Joel Schick   Morrow, 1995   GRADES 4–5

The children are finally able to return to their classroom on the thirtieth floor at Wayside School. Just when they are settling in, Mrs. Jewls, their teacher, takes maternity leave. Thus begins a string of odd substitute teachers, including one who steals children's voices through his third nostril.

3

Where Are Your Poetry Books?

Candy Corn by James Stevenson
Greenwillow, 1999   GRADES K–2

> Fifty-four short and humorous poems illustrated by the author. In "Peanuts," first there was one peanut, then two, then some more and then they were gone.

Cat up a Tree: A Story in Poems by Anne Isaacs
Illustrated by Stephen Mackey   Dutton, 1998   GRADES K–5

> The story of a cat up a tree unfolds one poem at a time. Each poem depicts a changing mood and voice as the girl, the cat, the fireman, the cat-catcher, the robin, the tree, the balloon lady, the box-car racer, the night, and the moon all have something to say.

Falling Up by Shel Silverstein
HarperCollins, 1996   GRADES K–5

> Author and illustrator Silverstein is, once again, the master of comical prose. In "Little Hoarse," a boy indicates that he is a little hoarse. Next thing he knows, he has a saddle on his back and children climbing up for a ride. In "The Monkey," Silverstein integrates numbers into the poem. A monkey was going 2 the store when he saw a banana 3. He eats green bananas and gets a tummy ache. On goes the poem until number 11.

From the Bellybutton of the Moon, and Other Summer Poems / Del ombligo de la luna, y otros poemas de verano by Francisco Alarcón   Illustrated by Maya Christina Gonzalez   Children's Book Press, 1998   GRADES 2–5

> Alarcon's bilingual collection celebrates the sounds and sights of summer from the perspective of a Mexican-American family living in Los Angeles.

The delights of long leisurely summer days lived out-of-doors can be shared by children in any circumstance.

Genie in the Jar by Nikki Giovanni
Illustrated by Chris Raschka   Henry Holt, 1996   GRADES K–3

> In a celebration of love and spirit, a young black girl is encouraged to take a note and spin it round and round. Being warned not to prick her finger, the girl spins notes on the Black loom, weaves the air around the Black loom, and makes the sky sing a song from the Black loom. Comfort and love abound in the simple text.

Hoops by Robert Burleigh
Illustrated by Stephen T. Johnson   Harcourt, Brace, 1997   GRADES K–5

> Action is the name of this game of basketball as poetic words describe the ball, moving it down the court, dribbling, shooting, and making the basket. Simple yet strong and fast moving text is accentuated by the illustrations of Stephen T. Johnson.

Hopscotch Love: A Family Treasury of Love Poems by Nikki Grimes
Illustrated by Melodye Rosales
Lothrop, Lee & Shepard, 1999   GRADES K–5

> Containing twenty-two poems, this collection deals with every kind of love in the African-American community. In "Christmas Valentine," a young boy asks his mother what she wants for Christmas. Upon hearing that his mother only wants him, he sneaks into her sewing room and glues velvet, ribbon, and lace together to make her a Christmas valentine.

Hush! A Thai Lullaby by Minfong Ho
Illustrated by Holly Meade   Orchard, 1996   GRADES K–3

> In this rhyming and repetitive text, a mother warns different animals to hush, as her baby is sleeping nearby. A mosquito, a lizard, a black cat, a mouse, a frog, a pig, a duck, a monkey, a buffalo, and an elephant all threaten to wake the baby. When all is quiet, the mother dozes. Nothing is stirring, that is, nothing except the baby.

I Am the Cat by Alice Schertle
Illustrated by Mark Buehner   Lothrop, Lee & Shepard, 1999   GRADES K–3

> Poems about a clever, demanding, incredible cat. The outrageous Sophie, the dog-taunting cat, thought she was invincible, as no dog could reach

her. But along comes a mongrel that can jump, and Sophie has taunted the dogs for the very last time. There are hidden animals in every illustration.

I Never Told and Other Poems by Myra Cohn Livingston
Illustrated by Brian Pinkney   Margaret K. McElderry, 1992   GRADES 3–5

A collection of twenty-five original poems on everyday things using succinct yet meaningful text. In "The Dream," the reader experiences growing wings and flying. In "This Book Is Mine," he or she understands quite clearly the meaning of "I found another me."

Insectlopedia by Douglas Florian
Harcourt, Brace, 1998   GRADES K–3

Illustrated by the author, this book contains twenty-one short poems about insects. Titles include "The Dragonfly," who is the demon of the skies and "The Inchworm," arched and ready for a stroll. In "The Termites," Florian builds a mound of words which grows just as deep underground.

Neighborhood Odes by Gary Soto
Illustrated by David Diaz   Harcourt, Brace, 1992   GRADES 3–6

Soto's funny, yet evocative, poems celebrate everyday things in the lives of children, such as tennis shoes, little brothers, snow cones, and playing in a water sprinkler. Each poem delightfully hones in on an extraordinary detail to be found in an ordinary object, place, or person.

Pish Posh, Said Hieromymus Bosch by Nancy Willard
Illustrated by Leo and Diane Dillon
Harcourt, Brace, Jovanovich, 1991   GRADES 3–5

Hieromymus Bosch, an artist who lived in the middle fifteenth and early sixteenth centuries, was known for creating odd creatures in his art. Tired of looking after his odd creatures everyday, and hearing "pish posh" from Hieromymus Bosch, the housekeeper leaves the menagerie. When she opens her suitcase, she finds that she has taken some of the creatures with her. Soon, she returns to the household of Hieromymus Bosch on condition that she will no longer have to do all the work.

A Pizza the Size of the Sun by Jack Prelutsky
Illustrated by James Stevenson   Greenwillow, 1996   GRADES K–5

In this collection of humorous poetry, Prelutsky once again tickles the funny bones of students of all ages. In "It's Hard to Be an Elephant," an elephant complains that it is so big that it can't attend the cinema or board a bus. And worst of all, it can't find socks or underwear that fit exactly right!

Sad Underwear . . . And Other Complications by Judith Viorst
Illustrated by Richard Hull   Atheneum, 1995   GRADES 4–7

In this companion to *If I Were in Charge of the World and Other Worries,* Viorst deals with the first day of school, fairy tales, and moms and dads. In "What Dads Do," dads do everything from making bookshelves to explaining electricity. Happiness is soon replaced by yearning when the last line states, "I wish I still had one." The short poem "Item of Information" explains succinctly what a disgrace is and will be secretly understood by many.

4

Where Are Your Fairy Tales?
(Picture Books)

Canary Prince by Eric Jon Nones
Farrar, Straus, & Giroux, 1991   GRADES K–3

A king's daughter is locked in a castle deep in the forest because of her jealous stepmother. Day after day, the girl sits by a window looking down at the forest. One day she spots the son of a neighboring king passing along the castle trail and the two unite in gaze. When a mysterious book appears in the girl's room, she turns the page forward and the prince changes into a canary and flies into her room. When the girl turns the page back, the canary turns back into a prince. When her jealous stepmother finds out about the tryst, she plans revenge. Using the book and her own skills, the girl is able to foil her stepmother's plans.

Cendrillon: A Caribbean Cinderella by Robert San Souci
Illustrated by Brian Pinkney   Simon & Schuster, 1998   GRADES K–5

Set on the Caribbean island of Martinique, this Cinderella story is narrated by the nannin', or godmother. When Cendrillon's mother dies, her father marries a woman who works Cendrillon as a serving girl. When Cendrillon hears that Monsieur Thibault's son, Paul, is having a fet', she wishes she could attend. Of course her stepmother and stepsister are attending, but Cendrillon must stay home. Then, her nannin' has an idea. With a wand of mahogany given to her by her dying mother, the nannin' transforms Cendrillon into a proper young lady and herself into a chaperone. Once at the fet', Cendrillon dances with Paul and captures his heart. Unfortunately, when the clock strikes midnight, Cendrillon must depart in haste, leaving Paul to search for the owner of the pink slipper.

Girl in the Golden Bower by Jane Yolen
Illustrated by Jane Dyer   Little, Brown, 1994   GRADES K–3

In this original fairy tale, a queen has died, the king has disappeared, and a beast lives in the uninhabited castle. When a woodsman finds a frail young woman wandering in the wood, he takes her in, feeds her, clothes her, and falls in love with her. Eventually, they have a daughter they call Aurea. Five years later, a sorceress comes to the woodsman's cottage searching for a charm. Finding none, the sorceress kills the parents, leaving Aurea to fend for herself. Left with a magic comb, Aurea befriends the animals of the forest and combs the tangles from their fur. Soon the sorceress realizes that the comb is the charm. How will Aurea escape the sorceress and keep her comb?

The Girl Who Loved Caterpillars by Jean Merrill
Illustrated by Floyd Cooper   Philomel, 1992   GRADES 1–4

Izumi is unhappy with her privileged life as the daughter of a nobleman in the Emperor's court. She has no interest whatsoever in traditionally feminine pursuits, nor does she aspire to grow up to be a lady-in-waiting, as most girls in her position do. Instead she'd rather spend her days studying the insects and caterpillars the village boys bring to her. This captivating story, first written by an anonymous twelfth-century Japanese writer, has a startlingly modern tone and is beautifully illustrated by Floyd Cooper.

The Girl Who Spun Gold by Virginia Hamilton
Illustrated by Leo and Diane Dillon   Blue Sky/Scholastic, 2000 GRADES K–4

An elegant retelling of a West Indian version of "Rumpelstiltskin" is well matched by Leo and Diane Dillon's stunning, detailed, gold-tinted illustrations. After Quashiba's mother brags that her daughter can spin an entire field into gold, a greedy king marries the young woman and locks her into a room, ordering her to fill it with gold. Enter a tiny monster called Lit'mahn who promises to do the work in exchange for Quashiba's own life—unless, of course, she can guess his true name.

Irish Cinderlad by Shirley Climo
Illustrated by Loretta Krupinski   HarperCollins, 1996   GRADES K–4

Becan is an Irish lad with very large feet. When he is thirteen years old, his mother dies and his father marries a woman with three daughters. The stepsisters treat Becan poorly and he is sent to the fields to be a herd boy. When Becan and the notorious speckled bull become friends, the stepsisters have the bull slaughtered. When the speckled bull dies, Becan takes its tail, which has special powers, and uses it to fight a giant and to rescue a princess from a dragon, losing his boot in the process. Thinking it is the end of his adventures, Becan returns home, only to have an unexpected visitor prove otherwise.

Lily and the Wooden Bowl by Alan Schroeder
Illustrated by Yoriko Ito   Doubleday, 1994   GRADES K–5

Lily is a beautiful but poor girl who lives in long-ago Japan with her grandmother. Before her grandmother dies, the old woman gives Lily two things, a rice paddle and a folded paper crane. Lily now must work in the rice fields, and her paper crane protects her from the torments of the other workers. When Lily accepts an offer to work inside a luxurious house, she is grateful but unhappy. Cruel Matsu, the wife of the house, hates Lily. Then Matsu's son, Kumaso, comes home from the city and he is instantly drawn to Lily. As hard as Matsu tries to keep them apart, Lily and Kumaso fall in love and must battle the evil Matsu in order to stay together.

Ouch! A Tale from Grimm retold by Natalie Babbit
Illustrated by Fred Marcellino   HarperCollins, 1998   GRADES K–5

When a king hears a prophecy that a baby boy born with a birthmark shaped like a crown will marry a princess, the king tries to dispose of the boy down the river. After floating for miles, the baby boy is found by a childless miller, who names him Marco. When Marco turns sixteen, the king finds out his true identity and the prophecy is uncovered. The king orders him killed, but it is love at first sight for Marco and the Princess and they are married. The king is furious and sends Marco on a journey that tests his strength and bravery.

Rapunzel by Paul O. Zelinsky
Dutton, 1997   GRADES K–3

In this unique version of Rapunzel, a childless couple loses their only child to their neighbor, a sorceress. When the child, named Rapunzel, turns twelve, the sorceress locks her away in a tower. Years later, a prince finds her hiding place and falls in love with Rapunzel. When their forbidden love is discovered, the sorceress punishes them both. Rapunzel, preganant, is forced to live in the wild country with no one to look after her. The prince falls from the tower, is blinded, and wanders the countryside like a vagabond. A year later, the prince hears Rapunzel's voice and they are reunited. Her tears cure his blindness and they live happily ever after.

Ugly Duckling adapted by Jerry Pinkney
Morrow, 1999   GRADES K–3

When a mother duck noticed that one of her eggs was bigger than the others, she thought nothing of it. But the hatchling looked nothing like her or the other ducklings. In fact, it was the ugliest duckling she had ever seen. As the duckling got older, the taunting and teasing increased and he ran away. When spring arrived, the duckling saw a flock of beautiful birds and decided to follow them. Not only did he learn that he could fly, he also discovered where he belonged.

Wind Child by Shirley Rousseau Murphy
Illustrated by Leo and Diane Dillon   HarperCollins, 1999   GRADES 3–5

In this original fairy tale, a child named Resshie, born of the wind and a mortal woman, grows up wild and dreaming about her father and mother. When Resshie is grown, she is sent alone into the world, and she weaves rough cloth in order to make a living. Then she captures the wind in her weaving, and the beautiful cloth attracts people from far and wide to buy her creations. Eventually Resshie must use her weaving skills and her ability to understand the wind when a handsome prince appears at her door.

5

Where Are Your Fairy Tales?
(Chapter Books)

Ella Enchanted by Gail Carson Levine
HarperCollins, 1997   GRADES 4–6

It's bad enough to be stuck at school with a horrible classmate like Hattie, but to suddenly find yourself her stepsister would be much worse. Such is Ella's plight. To complicate matters, Lucinda the Fairy has given Ella the gift of obedience, a secret Hattie quickly discovers. Though Prince Char, who shares her interest in languages and sliding down banisters, would marry her if she'd only say "yes," she knows that she would be a danger to him, saddled as she is with her "gift." Love wins in the end, and much banister sliding ensues.

Fairy's Mistake by Gail Carson Levine
Illustrated by Mark Elliott   HarperCollins, 1999   GRADES 4–6

When Rosella gives an old woman a drink at the well, she is unaware that it is the fairy Ethelinda. As her reward, jewels spill out of Rosella's mouth every time she speaks. But when Rosella's selfish twin sister Myrtle sees the jewels, she wants some of her own. Myrtle goes to the well and waits for a stranger, any stranger that might be the fairy in disguise. A knight asks for a drink of water, and Myrtle rudely declines. Instead of getting a reward, Myrtle is punished. Whenever she opens her mouth, insects and snakes slither out. But all is not just, and the girls must use their gifts and punishments to set things right.

Ghost Fox by Lawrence Yep
Scholastic, 1994   GRADES 3–5

Little Lee accidentally bumps into a man on the street and the man tells him that he will be sorry. Soon after, Little Lee's father goes on a trading trip down the river, leaving Little Lee to take care of his mother. When Little Lee hears scratching at the door at night, his mother tells him it's a rat and they put out poison. But Little Lee is not so sure, especially when his mother starts behaving strangely. Using his own cunning, Little Lee rescues his mother from the ghost fox.

Handful of Beans by Jeanne Steig
Illustrated by William Steig   HarperCollins, 1998   GRADES K–5

Clever retelling of six fairy tales with rhyming text. The stories include those of "Rumpelstiltskin," who has a mean temper; "Beauty and the Beast"; "Hansel and Gretel"; "Little Red Riding Hood," who takes a custard pie to her granny; "The Frog Prince," who refused to give up; and "Jack and the Beanstalk."

Happily Ever After by Anna Quindlen
Illustrated by James Stevenson   Viking, 1997   GRADES 2–4

Kate is a tomboy through and through. Except, that is, when she needs a change. That's when she picks up a book of fairy tales and dreams of becoming a princess. When Kate receives a special Eddie Bestelli baseball mitt, she doesn't know just how special it is until she makes a wish and finds herself in a tower wearing a dress and a crown on her head. She is a princess! But Kate learns that being a princess is not all it's made out to be and eventually whispers into her Eddie Bestelli mitt that she wants to go home.

Prince of the Pond by Donna Jo Napoli
Illustrated by Judith Byron Schachner   Dutton, 1992   GRADES 4–6

When a prince finds himself turned into a frog, he doesn't know what to do until he meets a female frog who teaches him the way of frogs. She teaches him to jump like a frog and to eat insects and he teaches her compassion and friendship. Known now as Pin, the prince sets out to live a new life with his new friend. Soon, they mate and have tadpoles. But one day, Pin is kissed by a human princess and turns back into a real prince. His frog family must then cope with the fact that their father will never be coming back.

Rose Daughter by Robin McKinley
Greenwillow, 1997   GRADES 5–8

Beauty lives in exile at Rose Cottage with her father and two sisters, Jeweltongue and Lionheart. Beauty loves gardening and faithfully tends the rosebushes in the garden. But she is haunted by a recurring dream, or is it a nightmare? After a journey to the city, Beauty's father brings a rose as a gift. But the rose has a price, and Beauty goes to live with the Beast. Thus begins Beauty's adventure living in an enchanted castle where roses bloom on leafless bushes.

Shoemaker's Boy by Joan Aiken
Illustrated by Victor G. Ambrus   Simon & Schuster, 1994   GRADES 2–6

Jem's mother is sick so his father, the shoemaker, leaves him to care for her and the shop while he sets out on a pilgrimage to the Holy City of St. James. One night several mysterious visitors come, one of whom brings the key to Jem's mother's health.

Well of the Wind by Alan Garner
Illustrated by Herve Blondon   DK, 1998   GRADES 2–4

When a fisherman finds two children at sea, he takes them home and raises them as his own. There is a star on each child's forehead, and the fisherman makes them silk headbands to hide the stars. But the fisherman dies, leaving the brother and sister to fend for themselves. One day, a witch from the woods visits the hut and she brings both riches and trouble. Eventually, the children learn their true identity.

6

Do You Have Any Other Books Like *The True Story of the Three Little Pigs?*
(Fractured Fairy Tales)

Bubba the Cowboy Prince: A Fractured Texas Tale by Helen
Ketteman   Illustrated by James Warhola   Scholastic, 1997   GRADES K–3

> Bubba lives on a ranch with his wicked stepfather and two hateful step-
> brothers. Even though Bubba does all the chores, he never complains
> because he loves ranching. One day Miz Lurleen, the prettiest and richest
> gal in the county, decides to find herself a fellow. So she plans a ball, invit-
> ing all the ranchers in Texas. With the help of a fairly godmother, Bubba
> arrives at the ball and just before midnight is able to dance with Miz
> Lurleen. Unfortunately for Bubba, the clock strikes twelve in the middle
> of a do-si-do. Bubba runs, leaving behind an old, stinky cowboy boot. But
> Miz Lurleen doesn't care. She won't be happy until she finds its owner.

Cinder Edna by Ellen Jackson
Illustrated by Kevin O'Malley   Lothrop, Lee & Shepard, 1994   GRADES K–3

> Cinder Edna is a cheerful sort of girl. Unlike Cinderella, she doesn't feel
> sorry for herself just because she has to work for her wicked stepmother
> and stepsisters. In fact, she has learned a thing or two, like how to make
> tuna casserole. When the king announces that he is giving a ball, her step-
> sisters order Cinder Edna around as they prepare for the big event. But
> unlike Cinderella, Cinder Edna doesn't believe in fairy godmothers and
> uses her own money and public transportation to get to the ball. While
> she finds Prince Randolph boring, she finds his younger brother Rupert
> appealing. He even likes tuna casserole. When the clock strikes twelve,
> both Cinderella and Cinder Edna run for the door. Left behind for Ran-
> dolph and Rupert are two shoes, a glass slipper and a loafer. The brothers
> search the countryside until they find the owners. And unlike Cinderella,
> Cinder Edna lives contently ever after.

Cinderella Penguin or, The Little Glass Flipper by Janet Perlman
Viking, 1992   GRADES K–3

A penguin named Cinderella lived with her stepmother and two selfish and lazy stepsisters. One day the Penguin Prince announced that he was giving a costume ball. Of course, the stepsisters just had to go, and Cinderella had to help them prepare for the big event. In this penguin version of Cinderella, it is a glass flipper that leads the prince to his penguin.

The Cowboy and the Black-Eyed Pea by Tony Johnston
Illustrated by Warren Ludwig   Putnam, 1992   GRADES K–3

Farethee Well is rich and beautiful. When her father was dying, he told her to find a real cowboy who is sensitive and will love her for herself. So when callers start coming to ask for her hand, Farethee Well hides a black-eyed pea under their saddle blankets then sends them out to ride the range. If they came back fresh as a Texas morning, they are rejected. Potential suitors come and go, but not one is troubled by the black-eyed pea until a young man arrives seeking shelter from a storm.

Dinorella: A Prehistoric Fairy Tale by Pamela Duncan Edwards
Illustrated by Henry Cole   Hyperion, 1997   GRADES K–3

Dora, Doris and Dinorella are dinosaurs. Dora and Doris are demanding and detrimental to Dinorella. They make Dinorella do all the dirty duties. One day, an invitation arrives. There is to be a dance at Duke Dudley's Den. The dreadful dinosaur duo doll themselves up for the dance while Dinorella, dejected, watches them depart. Suddently, a Fairydactyl appears. Dinorella is decked out in dazzling diamonds and destined for the dance. Just as Dinorella is descending upon Duke Dudley's Den, she hears a deafening disturbance. A deinonychus is doing a dastardly deed and Dinorella uses her diamond to foil the demon.

Fanny's Dream by Caralyn Buehner
Illustrated by Mark Buehner   Dial, 1996   GRADES K–3

Fanny, a sturdy girl living in Wyoming, dreams that she will marry a prince—or at least the mayor's son. So when she hears that the mayor is giving a ball, Fanny dresses in her best clothes and goes out into the garden to wait for her fairy godmother. The voice she hears isn't a fairy, it is Heber Jesen, a short but pleasant farmer who wants to marry Fanny.

Goldilocks and the Three Hares by Heidi Petach
Putnam, 1995   GRADES K–3

Mama hare burns the oatmeal and the three hares decide to eat out for breakfast. Meanwhile, Goldilocks falls into their hole, and a robber gang of weasels sneak in after her. Goldilocks tries out the burnt oatmeal, the chairs, and papa hare's waterbed. Upon returning home, the hares realize that someone has broken into their hole and call 911. Goldilocks is found and the weasels are captured. At the bottom of each page spread, mice provide commentary on the adventure.

Little Red Riding Hood: A Newfangled Prairie Tale by Lisa Campbell Ernst
Simon & Schuster, 1995   GRADES K–3

Once there was a little girl who, when riding her bike, always wore a red jacket with a red hood. Of course, everyone had to call her Little Red Riding Hood. One day, Little Red Riding Hood sets out to take her grandma some muffins and lemonade. Across the prairie Little Red Riding Hood rides, until she encounters a very hungry wolf who decides to beat Little Red Riding Hood to her grandmother's house. This wolf surely did not expect such a strong grandmother!

Rumpelstiltskin's Daughter by Diane Stanley
Morrow, 1997   GRADES K–4

When the miller's daughter is given the impossible task of weaving straw into gold, Rumpelstiltskin arrives to help her out. And instead of marrying the king, she marries Rumpelstiltskin. They and their daughter live happily together far away from the palace. But one day the King kidnaps the girl and demands that she make gold from straw. But Rumpelstiltskin's daughter has a plan. She fools the king into helping the poor and—instead of marrying the king—becomes prime minister.

Sleepless Beauty by Frances Minters
Illustrated by G. Brian Karas   Viking, 1996   GRADES K–4

This Sleeping Beauty version has a rock and rhyme twist. In rhymed text, the parents of Little Beauty throw a party. Unfortunately, the witch from down the block is overlooked and does not receive an invitation. In anger, she crashes the party and gives Little Beauty a big kiss for her birthday and then a curse. Little Beauty will, on her fourteenth birthday, be pricked by something sharp and made to sleep for a hundred years, after which a great rock star will awaken her. On her fourteenth birthday, Little Beauty plays a record and pricks her finger on the needle and the curse is activated. But not for long.

Stinky Cheese Man and Other Fairly Stupid Tales
by Jon Scieszka and Lane Smith   Viking, 1992   GRADES K–5

Ten fairly mixed-up tales introduced by Jack, the narrator. When the Little Red Hen inquires about a helper, Jack ignores her and introduces the stories. In the first story, Chicken Licken tells Ducky Lucky, Goosey Loosey, and Cocky Locky that the sky is falling. As they run to tell the President, Jack interrupts to tell them that he has forgotten the table of contents. They ignore him and meet Foxy Loxy just outside the airport. Foxy Loxy tricks them and leads them to his cave, where they are all crushed by the table of contents. In "The Princess and the Bowling Ball," the traditional pea is replaced by something bigger. Cinderumpelstiltkin really blows it, and the Stinky Cheese Man thinks his smell will save him.

Three Little Javelinas by Susan Lowell
Illustrated by Jim Harris   Northland, 1992   GRADES K–3

Three little javelinas lived in the Sonaran Desert in this southwestern and feminist version of the "Three Little Pigs." And while the first two javelinas' houses are destroyed by the coyote, the third little javelina builds her house out of adobe bricks. She welcomes her homeless brothers into her new house and locks the door. The coyote, hot on the brothers' trail, finds the house of the third javelina. Spying a stovepipe, the Coyote uses his magic to make himself very skinny. The third little javelina thinks fast and builds a fire in the stove. And Coyote the trickster thought it was hot outside!

Three Little Wolves and the Big Bad Pig by Eugene Trivizas
Illustrated by Helen Oxenbury   Margaret K. McElderry, 1993   GRADES K–3

Once upon a time, there were three cuddly wolves. When it was time for them to go out in the world, they were warned by their mother to watch out for the big bad pig. And while the pig could destroy houses of bricks, cement, and barbed wire, he had some trouble with the house of flowers.

The Three Pigs/Los Tres Cerdos: Nacho, Tito and Miguel
by Bobbi Salinas   Piñata Publications, 1999   Grades K–3

This bilingual recasting of "The Three Little Pigs" is set in the American Southwest and features Nacho the music lover, Tito the painter, and Miguel the computer nut and writer as the three pig brothers who have to face the big bad lobo, José. The illustrations include many humorous references to Chicano pop culture figures, including Rudy Galindo and San Elvis.

7

I Want to Read a Folktale, Legend, Myth, or Tall Tale

Bossy Gallito retold by Lucia M. Gonzalez
Illustrated by Lulu Delacre   Scholastic, 1994   GRADES K–5

> In English and Spanish, this is the story of a bossy rooster on his way to his cousin's wedding. Along the way, the gallito finds a piece of corn and it dirties his beak. When the gallito asks the grass to clean his beak, the grass says no. So he tells the goat to eat the grass. The goat says no. He tells the stick to hit the goat. The stick says no. He tells the fire to burn the stick. The fire says no. He tells water to put out the fire. The water says no. When he sees his friend the sun, the rooster asks him to dry the water. When the water overhears this, it quickly agrees to quench the fire. The fire agrees to burn the stick, the stick to hit the goat, the goat to eat the grass, and the grass to clean the gallito's beak. It does so, and the gallito hurries to his cousin's wedding.

First Strawberries: A Cherokee Story by Joseph Bruchac
Illustrated by Anna Vojtech   Dial, 1993   GRADES K–3

> The Creator in this Cherokee legend makes man and woman at the same time so that neither will be lonesome. They marry and live happily together. But one day, harsh words are spoken when the man finds that his wife has not yet prepared their meal. She becomes angry and leaves him, walking toward the sun with quick steps. Her husband follows her but he cannot keep up so he appeals to the sun for help. The sun creates several diversions until the woman's attention is finally attracted by strawberries. She forgives her husband, and to this day the Cherokee people are reminded that friendship and respect are as sweet as the taste of strawberries.

John Henry by Julius Lester
Illustrated by Jerry Pinkney   Dial, 1994   GRADES K–5

When John Henry is born, the animals come out of the woods to see him. To their surprise, John Henry starts growing and doesn't stop. Using his strength and creativity, John Henry encounters many adventures. Unfortunately, one of his challenges takes his life. Rumor has it that he is buried under the White House lawn while the president and first lady are sleeping.

La Cucaracha Martina: A Caribbean Folktale
retold by Daniel Moreton   Turtle Books, 1997   GRADES K–5

La Cucaracha Martina hates the noise of big city life. It hurts her tiny ears and keeps her awake at night. Sometimes, however, Martina is able to hear the most beautiful, gentle sound that she has ever heard. One day, Martina decides to search for the origin of the beautiful noise. On her journey, she meets many different animals, but none of them make the sound. Months later, when Martina can walk no more, she hears the sound. Once she finds the source of the beautiful sound, Martina never wants to live without it.

Legend of the Poinsettia retold by Tomie de Paola
Putnam, 1993   GRADES K–5

Lucida lives with her family in a small village in Mexico. She helps her mama at home and takes care of Paco and Lupe, her little brother and sister. When Padre Alvarez asks Lucida's mother to weave a new blanket for the figure of Baby Jesus, she is honored. On Christmas Eve, Lucida's mama becomes ill and Lucida must finish the blanket herself. But her attempt fails and the yarn is a tangled mess. Now her family won't have a gift to place on the manger. Lucida is ashamed and hides during the procession. But an old lady finds her and teaches her a valuable lesson about giving.

Mike Fink: A Tall Tale retold by Steven Kellogg
Morrow, 1992   GRADES K–4

Mike Fink, born near the Allegheny Mountains, is no ordinary infant. When he is two days old, he runs away from home and joins a gang of frogs. Soon, Mike learns that he wants to be a keelboatman. After Mike proves himself and becomes King of the Keelboatmen, steamboats begin threatening his life and livelihood and he finds himself in a match with

Captain Blathersby, a steamboat skipper. Mike Fink once again comes out on top.

Mouse Match by Ed Young
Harcourt, Brace, 1997   GRADES K–3

> In this folktale from China, a mouse family lives in a mouse village with their wonderful daughter. Wanting everything for their daughter the parents ask the sun, the wind, the clouds, and others what will bring her happiness. After asking everyone who is the most powerful, they learn that when they need answers they just have to look within themselves.

Robber Baby: Stories from the Greek Myths by Anne Rockwell
Greenwillow, 1994   GRADES 3–5

> This is a collection of fifteen tales from Greek mythology succinctly written for children. In "The Robber Baby," clever baby Hermes steals a herd of cows while his mother Maia sleeps. When Apollo finds his cows missing, he confronts Maia who denies the accusation, but Hermes is caught with a lyre made from the hide of two cows. Soon Apollo is spellbound by the sound of the lyre. Hermes trades the lyre to Apollo for the stolen cows. But Hermes wants more and is just clever enough to get it.

Secret Room by Uri Shulevitz
Farrar, Straus, & Giroux, 1993   GRADES K–3

> A king traveling through the desert met a man with a gray head and a black beard. When the king asked why, the man answered that his head was older than his beard. The king, pleased with the reply, ordered the man to secrecy until he had seen the king's face ninety-nine times. This old man, who eventually becomes an advisor to the king, is able to teach the king and his chief counselor many lessons about cleverness, humility, and honesty.

Tops and Bottoms adapted by Janet Stevens
Harcourt, Brace, 1995   GRADES K–3

> Once there was a wealthy bear who wanted to do nothing but sleep. Down the road lived a clever hare. But due to some unfortunate dealings, the hare was in bad financial shape. So the hare and his wife cooked up a plan to be business partners with the bear. The hare proposed that he plant and harvest a crop in the bear's field. Then they would split the profit right down the middle. But will this deal be a good one for everyone?

When Birds Could Talk and Bats Could Sing by Virginia Hamilton
Illustrated by Barry Moser   Blue Sky, 1996   GRADES K–5

The eight stories in this collection were first recorded by Martha Young (1862–1941), the daughter of a wealthy plantation owner. She collected many of the stories from former slaves who later became paid house servants to her family after the Civil War. The stories were rewritten for children by Virginia Hamilton.

Why Meat Loves Salt by Nina Jaffe
Illustrated by Louise August   Henry Holt, 1998   GRADES K–5

A rabbi has three daughters, Reyzeleh, the oldest, Khaveleh, the middle, and Mireleh, the youngest. The rabbi loves his daughters very much but he wonders how much they love him. So he asks Reyzeleh how much she loves him. She tells him that she loves him as much as diamonds. The middle daughter Khaveleh tells him that she loves him as much as gold and silver. Mireleh, the youngest, responds that she loves him the way meat loves salt. Angry, the rabbi drives her from the house. Eventually Mireleh is able to show her father the meaning of her response.

Zomo the Rabbit: A Trickster Tale from West Africa
by Gerald McDermott   Harcourt, Brace, 1992   GRADES K–5

Zomo the rabbit is very clever, but he wants more than cleverness; he wants wisdom. The Sky God tells him to do three things and Zomo does everything. He is indeed clever. He has courage and good sense but no caution. Now Zomo must watch out.

8

Where Are Your Science Fiction Books?

The Ear, The Eye and the Arm by Nancy Farmer
Orchard, 1994   GRADES 5–8

> After three children escape from their high-security home in this story set in Zimbabwe in 2194, their parents hire a detective team to find them. The Ear, the Eye, and the Arm, as the detectives call themselves, aren't very good at detecting but they do have psychic abilities that aid them in their search for the missing children.

Giver by Lois Lowry
Houghton Mifflin, 1993   GRADES 5–8

> Jonas lives in a place that has no crime, no starvation, and no war. It's a place where everyone wears the same clothes, lives in the same houses, and eats the same food. Jonas is content until he reaches his twelfth year, the year he and the other Twelves are assigned their jobs in life. When Jonas is chosen to be the next Receiver, it is a great honor. But Jonas must spend his time receiving memory from the past from his teacher, the Giver. In the passing of the memories, Jonas for the first time experiences love and hate and starvation and pain. The more memories he receives from the Giver, the more he doubts his utopian society. Can he change it?

Great Interactive Dream Machine by Richard Peck
Dial, 1996   Grades 4–6

> Josh Lewis and his best and only friend Aaron Zimmerman live in the same apartment building. But, life isn't easy for the two boys as they avoid the bullies at their school, deal with their parents, and face Miss Mather, the old woman who lives below Josh. When Josh and Aaron find themselves walking Nanky-Poo, Miss Mather's dog, they also find that

Miss Mather is not mean but lonely. And when the friends have to make an oral report in summer school, Miss Mather comes to the rescue and is reunited with an old flame.

Hermit Thrush Sings by Susan Butler
DK, 1999   GRADES 5–7

A meteor has hit the earth, and the world no longer exists as it was. An oppressive government rules the villages, guarding the human inhabitants from the mutants known as birmba. In this Cinderella story with a twist, Leora, an orphan, lives with her stepmother and stepsister who plan to send her to an institution for the defective. She flees from her proposed fate and searches for her sister who disappeared years before. When she comes face to face with the ferocious birmba Leora realizes, through touch, that they are not dangerous. With only a birmba as companion, Leora finds her rebel sister and aids in the uprising of the people.

I Left My Sneakers in Dimension X by Bruce Coville
Illustrated by Katherine Coville   Pocket Books, 1994   GRADES 4–6

When Rod Allbright and his cousin Elspeth are kidnapped by Smorkus Flinders, a monster from Dimension X, their summer vacation takes on a new outlook. Rod is being used as a pawn to attract Smorkus Flinders' enemy, Captain Grakker. But Grakker and the rest of the crew of the *Ferkel* are friendly to Rod. Rod and Elspeth are rescued but the *Ferkel* is damaged and Rod, Elspeth, and the crew must bail out. In search of assistance, the crew meets a shape shifter. The shape shifter takes them to see Ting Wongovia, an alien trained in the Mental Arts. A plan made for defeating Smorkus Flinders backfires. Now it's up to Rod to defeat the monster and save Earth.

Ned Feldman, Space Pirate by Daniel Pinkwater
Macmillan, 1994   GRADES 2–4

When Ned Feldman hears a noise under his kitchen sink, he is surprised to find a space pirate. Captain Lumpy Lugo whisks Ned off to space. Although Captain Lumpy Lugo, also known as Bugbeard, is not a brave pirate, Ned is indeed excited. When they land on a planet, they meet giant chickens that they ride like horses. But when they meet a Yeti, Ned and Bugbeard run for their lives back to the spaceship. Soon, Bugbeard takes Ned back to the kitchen sink, and Ned has something to draw pictures of.

Off the Road by Nina Bawden
Clarion, 1998   GRADES 5–9

It's 2036 and Tom lives with his parents and grandfather inside the wall
that protects them from the dangerous natural world. When Tom's
grandfather escapes to avoid being killed at age sixty-five, Tom travels
with him outside and discovers a world free of the restrictions he has
always known.

Star Hatchling by Margaret Bechard
Puffin, 1997   GRADES 4–7

Shem and his sister Cheko find a fallen star in the forest. Hanna is the
human "hatchling" they find and plan to keep. But Hanna wants to get
back to her space pod and go home. This story switches back and forth
between the point of view of Shem and Cheko encountering a human
and that of Hanna encountering the "aliens."

9

What Are Some
Good Fantasy Books?

Clockwork by Philip Pullman
Illustrated by Leonid Gore   Scholastic, 1998   GRADES 4+

The folks at the White Horse tavern are ready for a splendid evening of terror when their local writer starts to read from his latest scary story. When the story suddenly comes to life right in the inn, Fritz bolts, a little girl named Gretl gives her heart to a prince made of silver, and a clockmaker's apprentice forfeits his life to a magical figure named Sir Ironsoul.

Harry Potter and the Sorcerer's Stone by J. K. Rowling
Illustrated by Mary Grandpre   Scholastic, 1999   GRADES 4+

Poor Harry is an orphan, living with his only remaining family, the horrible Dursleys. All his life he's been told that his parents died in a car accident but the truth is, they were a witch and a wizard and quite famous in the magic world. He learns the truth on his eleventh birthday, the same day he learns he has been accepted to Hogwarts, the famous wizard academy. When school starts Harry finds himself immersed in a new world, where Quidditch is the sport of choice and classes in Charms, Potions, and the Dark Arts are taught. With the help of his friends Ron and Hermione he also battles the evil Lord Voldemort, who killed his parents.

Heavenward Path by Kara Dalkey
Harcourt, Brace, 1998   Grades 4–6

Fujiwara no Mitsuko only wants to be left alone to study the holy sutras, but a ghost demands that she fulfill a rashly made promise. She must repair a shrine in the mountains before her father can marry her off to the Crown Prince. In a world where the beings of folklore and mythology are real she turns to her friend Goraun, a member of the trickster class of demons called tengu. Together with the priest Dento they fulfill her promise and make a bargain with the Lord of Death.

The Imp That Ate My Homework by Laurence Yep
Illustrated by Benrei Huang   HarperCollins, 1998   GRADES 3–5

The nasty green imp not only eats Jim's homework, but gets him into all kinds of trouble at home and at school. Why is the imp bothering with him at all? As Jim learns, his cranky grandfather is the reincarnation of Chung Kuei, the legendary Chinese imp-fighter, and the imp has come to seek revenge. Jim's grandfather joins him in a series of funny misadventures in an attempt to vanquish the imp once and for all.

Iron Ring by Lloyd Alexander
Dutton, 1997   GRADES 4–6

Tamar, King of Sundari, shouldn't have gambled with the stranger, but he did. Now he's lost his kingdom and probably his life. As a member of the warrior caste it is beneath him to renege on a debt of honor, so he starts on a journey that will take him to his death. Along the way he befriends a troublesome monkey, a beautiful goatherd, and a forlorn eagle who is searching for the magical Fire Flower, a gem of unspeakable power.

Jane on Her Own: A Catwings Tale by Ursula K. Le Guin
Illustrated by S. D. Schindler   Orchard, 1999   GRADES 2–4

The cats with wings are back in this fourth story from noted fantasy writer Ursula Le Guin. In this installment, Jane is bored with life on the farm where things are the same day in and day out. She takes off for a big adventure in the city, ignoring the warnings of the other cats about letting humans see her fly. When Jane arrives in the city, she is lonely. She cannot find a friend anywhere. She dives into an open window only to be caged and displayed by a sweet but misunderstanding man. Jane soon escapes to find her mother and her new home.

Moorchild by Eloise McGraw
Margaret K. McElderry, 1996   GRADES 5–7

Mogl is different. Even though she lives with the Folk, she doesn't quite fit in. Her mother was Folk and her father was human. She is sent to the human world as a changeling, a Folk exchanged for a human child. Mogl is renamed Saaski and lives like a human. But her grandmother, Old Bess, knows that something is wrong. Being different is hard for Saaski as the village children taunt and tease her. Saaski finds peace and happiness on the moor with her only friend, Tam. When illness and death of livestock occur in the village, Saaski is held responsible. With no hope of returning to her human family, she takes matters into her own hands.

Outcast of Redwall by Brian Jacques
Illustrated by Allan Curless   Philomel, 1996   GRADES 5–7

This installment of the history of Redwall Abbey finds the mousemaid, Bryony, fostering Veil, the ferret son of the evil warlord Swartt Sixclaw. Like any doting mother of a young monster, she is blind to his faults and insists that there is good in the young ferret. She is almost proven wrong when Swartt returns with his horde of evil beasts and Veil leaves to join him. After many battles and losses Bryony is able to confront Veil and offer him one last chance to do right.

Perloo the Bold by Avi
Scholastic, 1998   GRADES 4–8

Perloo would much rather curl up with his books of Montmer history and mythology, but when Lucabara arrives at his home and demands that he accompany her to the deathbed of his old friend Jolaine, Granter of the Montmers, he must obey. When Jolaine declares him the new Granter and then dies, his troubles begin. Jolaine's son Berwig wants to be Granter and will stop at nothing to get his way. Perloo's fight for his life turns into a fight for the Montmer way of life, and the lessons he learns cannot be found in his precious books.

Searching for Dragons by Patricia Wrede
Harcourt, Brace, 1991   GRADES 4–6

In the second installment of the Enchanted Forest Chronicles Princess Cimorene, now Chief Cook and Librarian to the Dragon King Kazul, is in trouble. Mendanbar, King of the Enchanted Forest, has come to Kazul for help and Cimorene must finally admit that Kazul is missing. They join together with Morwen the Witch and Telemain the Magician to battle the Society of Wizards, who are plotting to steal the magic of the Enchanted Forest and kill the Dragon King.

The Secret of Platform 13 by Eva Ibbotson
Illustrated by Sue Porter   Dutton, 1998   GRADES 4–6

Under the old, unused Platform 13 of King's Cross Railway Station there is a grassy bump called a gump and a hidden door that opens for exactly nine days every nine years. The door leads to an island where people live peacefully among ogres and hags and dragons. On the island live a king and queen with a beautiful baby boy. Thus begins the story of the young prince who is carried through the gump only to be kidnapped by a rich, childless woman in search of a baby to call her own. Nine days and nine years later, a rescue team is dispatched to bring the boy back.

Skellig by David Almond
Delacorte, 1999   GRADES 4–6

Michael, who is still reeling from the birth of a seriously ill sister and a move to a new house, makes an astonishing discovery while exploring the new property. What he finds isn't a man, angel, or bird. He is simply Skellig, who is suffering from arthritis, but still relishes Chinese food and brown ale. As Michael and his new neighbor Mina, who has a passion for art, nature, and William Blake, nurse him back to health they realize there is something odd about Skellig's shoulders. Skellig eventually moves on, leaving Michael and Mina to ponder the mystery of his existence.

Thief by Megan Whalen Turner
Greenwillow, 1996   GRADES 5–8

Gen stole the King of Sounis's ring and is serving his sentence in prison. When the King's magus offers him his freedom in exchange for stealing something else he accepts the offer. What they are stealing is Hamaithe's Gift, a mythical stone of great power, created by the old gods. Gen doesn't really believe the old stories, but he has ample motivation to succeed. Along with two apprentices and a soldier to guard Gen they make the long journey into the mountains. Things aren't always what they seem, and the magus and his apprentices soon learn some lessons about judging people by their appearances.

10

Do You Have Any Other Books Like *Magic Tree House?*
(Time Travel)

Blizzard Disaster by Peg Kehret
Simon & Schuster, 1998   GRADES 4–6

In 1940, Janis Huff is staggering home from school trying to find her way through a sudden blizzard that has hit their home in Minnesota. But when Ellie, Janis's little sister, goes outside to look for her imaginary squirrel, she too becomes a victim of the blizzard. Years later, Warren Spalding and Betsy Tyler have to write a report about the Armistice Day blizzard. Using Warren's grandfather's Instant Commuter and an old photograph of the blizzard, they find themselves in the middle a blinding snowfall. When Warren and Betsy hear a call for help, they rescue Ellie. How can they return to the present, since Ellie is from the past?

Dinosaur Habitat by Helen Griffith
Illustrated by Sonja Lamut   Greenwillow, 1998   GRADES 4–6

Ever since his mom got a job, Nathan has to be home after school to look after his little brother Ryan. Nathan and Ryan have to share a room and Nathan is not supposed to touch Ryan's things, especially his terrarium filled with plants and marsh soil and plastic dinosaurs. When Ryan returns from school one day with part of a fossil, the boys get into an argument and the fossil is thrown into the terrarium. The next thing the boys know, they have been transported back to the time when dinosaurs roamed the earth. After being chased by a diplodocus and a triceratops, Nathan is ready to go home. When Ryan finds a baby dinosaur, he is hesitant to give it up. But when the boys encounter a tyrannosaurus, they quickly find the fossil and themselves back home.

Honus and Me by Dan Gutman
Avon, 1997   GRADES 4–6

Joe Stoshack loves baseball. To earn some money, Joe cleans out the attic
for his elderly neighbor, Miss Young. In the attic, Joe finds an old Honus
Wagner baseball card. The card is worth thousands of dollars, and Joe
can't wait to get the money for his mother and himself. But something
happens when Joe holds the baseball card in his hand; the next thing he
knows Honus Wagner is sitting in his bedroom and Joe is wondering if he
can be transported back to 1909. Joe learns all about Honus and comes to
respect the man with funny ears and bow legs. When Joe's life is threatened over the valuable card, Miss Young comes to the rescue. She tears up
the card, making it worthless. But the lessons Joe learned are priceless.

Megan in Ancient Greece by Susan Korman
Illustrated by Bill Dodge   Magic Attic Press, 1998   GRADES 2–4

Megan and her friends are members of the Magic Attic Club. When the
girls find a gold key, they return it to its owner, Ellie Goodwin. Ellie invites
the girls to play in her attic and when they try on costumes of the past,
they are suddenly transported back in time. One rainy afternoon, Megan
finds that she has traveled over two thousand years into the past to an
agora, a Greek market. When she returns to the present, Megan finds
many things in modern day times to be thankful for, including her friends.

Orphan of Ellis Island by Elvira Woodruff
Scholastic, 1997   GRADES 5–8

Dominic is an orphan who has gone from one foster home to another.
When his fifth-grade class visits Ellis Island, Dominic is ashamed of not
knowing who his ancestors are. Soon, Dominic escapes from the taunting of his classmates to a closet where he decides to take a nap. When
Dominic wakes, he finds he has been transported back to 1908 Italy.
There he meets three poor and orphaned brothers, Francesco, Salvatore,
and Antonio. The brothers are being sent to America to be adopted by
two families. But when Salvatore suddenly dies, Dominic takes his place
on board the ship, the *New Amsterdam*. Upon arrival at Ellis Island,
Dominic takes a little nap and this time he awakens to the present.

The 13th Floor: A Ghost Story by Sid Fleischman
Illustrated by Peter Sis   Greenwillow, 1995   GRADES 4–6

When Buddy Stebbins' lawyer sister Liz receives a message from Abigail

Parson, an ancestor from the 1600s, she disappears the following day. Buddy suspects that Liz has gone to the thirteenth floor in an office building in San Diego. When Buddy gets to the thirteenth floor, he finds himself on a pirate ship headed by Captain Crackstone a.k.a. John Stebbins, in the middle of a stormy ocean. When Buddy does find Liz, she is defending Abigail Parsons against charges of witchcraft. But women were not lawyers in the seventeenth century and Buddy must defend Abigail with Liz's help. Eventually, Buddy and Liz make their way back home.

Tommy Traveller in the World of Black History by Tom Feelings
Black Butterfly/Writers and Readers, 1981   GRADES 3–6

When young Tommy seeks out the facts from black history, he's suddenly catapulted back in time where he witnesses first-hand dramatic events in the lives of Aesop, Crispus Attucks, Phoebe Fraunces, Frederick Douglass, Joe Louis, and Emmet Till. Feelings uses the style of Classic Comics to make the history accessible to young readers.

2095 by Jon Scieszka
Illustrated by Lane Smith   Viking, 1995   GRADES 3–5

The Time Warp Trio, Joe, Fred, and Sam, are at it again. This time they head for the future when they use Uncle Joe's magic book to transport them to 2095. During a class trip to the Natural History Museum, the trio visits the future and sees the 1990s as the past. They meet their great-grandchildren and ID checking robots and check out the price of pizza. With help from their great-grandchildren the trio evades the robots and return to the 1990s safe and sound.

Wizard's Map by Jane Yolen
Harcourt, Brace, 1999   GRADES 4–6

Twins Jennifer and Peter are not too excited when they travel to Scotland with their mother, father, and little sister Molly. They'd rather be home in Connecticut playing with their friends over the summer holiday. But things get exciting when they visit their Gran and Da's attic. Along with old-fashioned clothes, there is a game called Patience, something that their mother says the twins need more of. When four-year-old Molly finds a map she has no idea that she has unleashed the dark wizard, Michael Scot, from the past. With the help of three creatures, a dog, a dragon, and a unicorn, Jennifer is able to outwit the dark wizard and with her twin Peter, they free her family from the wizard's doom.

Your Mother Was a Neanderthal by Jon Scieszka
Viking, 1993   GRADES 4+

   The Time Warp Trio find themselves in the middle of an adventure in
   prehistoric times, where cave art is a form of graffiti and "rock" music
   takes on a whole new meaning. They land in the prehistoric era absolutely naked! After solving the problem of finding clothes, the boys have
   more worrisome things on their minds. How will they find their time-
   transporting book in this era when writing has yet to be invented? And
   do the cave girls really plan to eat them for supper?

Ziggy and the Black Dinosaurs: Lost in the Tunnel of Time
by Sharon Draper   Illustrated by Michael Bryant
Just Us Books, 1996   GRADES 3–5

   Ziggy, Rico, Rashawn, and Jerome, a.k.a. The Black Dinosaurs, discover
   an old tunnel that was once part of the Underground Railroad. When the
   only known entryway gets blocked, they must go deeper and deeper into
   the tunnel to find another way out, retracing the steps of escaped slaves
   from an earlier century.

11

I Want to Read
an Adventure Story

Adventures of Midnight Sun by Diane Lewis Patrick
Holt, 1997 GRADES 4–6

Thirteen-year-old Midnight Sun escapes from slavery on a Texas plantation and heads for Mexico, where he tastes true freedom. There he
befriends a group of vaqueros and joins a cattle drive going north to
Kansas, putting himself at great risk as a fugitive slave.

Adventures of Sparrowboy by Brian Pinkney
Simon & Schuster, 1997 GRADES 1–3

Henry is no ordinary newspaper carrier. In his own imagination, he's the
superhero, Sparrowboy, who comes to the rescue of helpless creatures in
the neighborhood that are being threatened by local bullies, big and
small. Appropriately illustrated using the style of superhero comics.

Bandit's Moon by Sid Fleischman
Illustrated by Joseph A. Smith   Greenwillow, 1998 GRADES 4–7

In the mid-1800s, twelve-year-old Annyrose Smith and her brother Lank
are orphaned when their mother dies during the voyage to the new U.S.
territory of California. The Gold Rush is in full swing, and greed and big-
otry abound. When they arrive in San Diego, a pickpocket steals all their
money. Then Annyrose sprains her ankle and Lank leaves her with a
horse thief named O.O. Mary. Being with O.O. Mary is the beginning of
Annyrose's adventures. When O.O. Mary leaves in haste, Annyrose, dis-
guised as a boy, begs Joaquin, the Mexican Robin Hood, to take her with
him. Joaquin agrees, under the condition that Annyrose teach him to
read English. Annyrose travels the state of California with Joaquin and

his men. Her conscience tells her that stealing is wrong but her heart has grown fond of this outlaw.

Cousins in the Castle by Barbara Brooks Wallace
Illustrated by Richard Williams   Atheneum, 1996   GRADES 4–6

When young Amelia Fairchild's father dies unexpectedly in Victorian London, Amelia is sent to New York with her stern Aunt Charlotte. Once she arrives in New York, Amelia is abandoned and then kidnapped. Readers will enjoy the many plot twists and fast-paced action.

Dolphin Treasure by Wayne Grover
Illustrated by Jim Fowler   Greenwillow, 1996   GRADES 3–5

In this fictionalized sequel to *Dolphin Adventure,* Wayne is diving for sunken treasure when a storm comes up and traps him in the water without a boat. It's Baby, the star of *Dolphin Adventure,* who rescues Wayne from hungry sharks and leads him back to shore.

Fear Place by Phyllis Reynolds Naylor
Atheneum, 1994   GRADES 5–7

In this story of intense sibling rivalry, Doug must put aside his fear of heights to save his brother lost on a camping trip. In this gripping adventure, Doug struggles to put aside his feelings about his brother in order to save him.

The Firework-Maker's Daughter by Philip Pullman
Illustrated by S. Saelig Gallagher   Levine, 1999   GRADES 4–6

Lila, daughter of a firework maker, tells her father she wants to become a master firework maker. When he tells her it is no job for a girl, she runs away to Mount Merapi to claim sulphur for making fireworks from the Fire-Fiend. Along the way, she faces many hardships with her friend Chulak and his talking white elephant, Hamlet.

Is Underground by Joan Aiken
Delacorte, 1992   GRADES 5–8

Is, short for Isabett, is the youngest sister of Dido Twite. Is makes a promise to her dying uncle to search for her cousin Arun and sets off on an adventure that will take her far from home. She learns that the children of London, including the King's son, have disappeared and Is must find out where they went. Following the clues, she boards the Playland

Express along with hundreds of other children. Soon, Is finds out the dreadful truth: the children are being taken to work in the coal mines. Able to escape, Is finds her great-grandfather and great-aunt and learns that her Uncle Roy, her father's brother, is behind all the villainy. With the help of her great-grandfather and great-aunt and the local doctor, Is foils Uncle Roy's plans and rescues the children.

Poppy by Avi
Illustrated by Brian Floca   Orchard, 1995   GRADES 4–6

Poppy, a deer mouse, is horrified when she sees her boyfriend, Ragweed, eaten by the mean owl Mr. Ocax. Mr. Ocax insists that he is king of Dimwood Forest and Poppy and her family must ask his permission to go anywhere. Due to a diminishing food supply, Poppy's father wants to move some of the family to a new place. But Mr. Ocax refuses and Poppy decides to take matters into her own hands. With the help of Ereth, the porcupine, Poppy is able to see for herself the false bravado of Mr. Ocax and the truth about porcupines.

Robber and Me by Josef Holub
Translated by Elizabeth D. Crawford   Holt, 1997   GRADES 6–8

Set in Germany in 1867, this is the story of Boniface Schroll, an orphaned boy who is sent to live with his strict uncle. He befriends the son of a man accused of being a robber and gets involved in a mystery to which he holds the key. Winner of the 1998 Mildred R. Batchelder Award.

Summer on Wheels by Gary Soto
Scholastic, 1995   GRADES 4–6

Hector and Mando take an eight-day bike ride from East Los Angeles to Santa Monica, stopping each night to stay with relatives along the way. A fast-paced, action-filled urban adventure story with lots of good-natured humor.

Titanic Crossing by Barbara Williams
Dial, 1995   Grades 4–8

Young Albert Trask sets sail on the Titanic with his sister and his mother. When the ship hits an iceberg and begins to sink, Albert must help his sister to the lifeboats, but is unable to find his mother. The author weaves many real passengers into the story and includes authentic details to give a strong feel for life on the ill-fated ship.

Winter Camp by Kirkpatrick Hill
Macmillan, 1993   GRADES 4–6

In this sequel to *Toughboy and Sister,* eleven-year-old John and his little
sister, Annie Laurie, learn the traditional ways of their Athabaskan heritage from an old woman named Natasha who's taken them in. She
teaches them how to survive in the wild through the cold Alaskan winter.
When Natasha is called away unexpectedly, John and Annie Laurie must
put all their survival skills to the test.

12

I Want to Read a Book about Kids Who Are Brave

Aani and the Tree Huggers by Jeanette Atkinson
Illustrated by Venantius Pinto   Lee & Low, 1995   GRADES 2–4

When men from the cities come to rural India to cut down the trees, young Aani joins the women in her village who successfully stop them by embracing individual trees. This picture story dramatizes the Chipko Andolan (Hug the Tree) Movement in northern India in the 1970s.

Barn by Avi
Orchard, 1994   GRADES 4–6

Nine-year-old Ben is summoned from school to find that his father is dying, stricken by what the doctor can only call a palsy. Yet Ben can't seem to give up on his father. As he and his brother and sister struggle to keep their father and the farm alive, Ben searches for a way to give his father the will to get better. While Ben and his siblings build a barn as a gift to their father, the father's health continues to deteriorate. After his father's death, Ben realizes that the barn was not only a gift to his father but also a gift to himself. Or was it a gift for everyone? Perhaps all of the above.

Captive by Joyce Hansen
Scholastic, 1994   GRADES 4–6

It's 1788, and Kofi is a proud Ashanti, son of a chief. Surely no one would dare capture the son of such an important man. But Kofi soon finds himself aboard a slave ship experiencing horrors that he would have thought unimaginable. He is sold, along with two other young boys, to a couple in Massachusetts who teach him to read and write and train him as a house servant. When the boys escape, they find refuge on a schooner.

Luckily, the schooner is owned by a free man, a Quaker, who helps them regain their freedom and dignity.

Earthquake Terror by Peg Kehret
Dutton, 1994   GRADES 4–6

Jonathan Palmer and his family plan to spend a quiet October day camping on Magpie Island in Northern California. When Jonathan's mother breaks her ankle, he is left alone on the island with his sister Abby, whose accident two years ago left her legs partially paralyzed, and their dog Moose. Soon the earth begins to shake and Jonathan, Abby, and Moose find themselves in the middle of an earthquake. It takes all of Jonathan's courage to find a way off the flooding island. The children manage to harness logs and float along until they are separated, when they must use all of their strength to survive.

The Ghost of Grania O'Malley by Michael Morpurgo
Viking, 1996   GRADES 4–6

Jessie Parsons doesn't give up her resolve to get to the top of the big hill one day. Climbing the hill is no easy task for Jessie, who has "lousy palsy," which keeps her off balance. But one day, Jessie does make it with the help of the ghost of Grania O'Malley. The ghost wants to save the Big Hill on their small Irish island from mining and potential destruction. With the help of her American cousin Jack and Grania O'Malley, Jessie uses all her courage to fight the islanders who support the mine and persuade them to save the hill.

Goodbye, Vietnam by Gloria Whelan
Knopf, 1992   GRADES 4–6

Mai and her family flee Vietnam to avoid police persecution, along with many other refugees who travel by boat to Hong Kong. Their arduous journey in an overcrowded boat ends with a lengthy stay in a refugee camp where they await word on whether they'll be allowed to enter another country or forced to return to Vietnam.

Grab Hands and Run by Frances Temple
Orchard, 1993   GRADES 4–6

Haunted by the suspicious disappearance of their father, twelve-year-old Felipe and his family must literally run for their lives from their native El Salvador, through Mexico and up into the United States, where they live as fugitives.

Hermit Thrush Sings by Susan Butler
DK, 1999 GRADES 5–7

See page 29 for a description of this book.

Holes by Louis Sachar
Farrar, Straus, & Giroux, 1998 GRADES 5+

Whenever bad luck struck, Stanley Yelnats's family blamed it on Stanley's "no-good-dirty-rotten-pig-stealing-great-great-grandfather." Now shy, overweight Stanley has been sent to a juvenile detention center in the middle of nowhere for being in the wrong place at the wrong time. Each day the boys are required to dig a five-by-five-foot hole in the merciless ground of a dried-up lake bed. Each day it's the same routine, until Stanley finds a gold tube. Learn how the truth is finally revealed and the wrong is righted. A great read dealing with relationships, greed, honesty, prejudice, bravery, and just plain luck.

The Imp That Ate My Homework by Laurence Yep
Illustrated by Benrei Huang   HarperCollins, 1998 GRADES 3–5

See page 32 for a description of this book.

Rock River by Bill Maynard
Putnam, 1998 GRADES 3–5

Luke's brother Robert died performing a daredevil stunt on the river. Now, Luke's mother is so overprotective that Luke feels he'll never have a chance to be brave. Then Luke and his friends are challenged by some girls to catch the biggest bass by the end of the summer. So begins their adventuresome search for the perfect bait. With the end of summer approaching, the boys have to come up with a solution fast. Unfortunately, rain disrupts their plans as it causes the river to overflow onto land. Disaster strikes when one of the boys is washed away on a makeshift raft. Is Luke brave enough to save him?

Stranded by Ben Mikaelsen
Hyperion, 1995 GRADES 4–6

Koby's life is in shambles. Nothing has been the same since she lost her foot in an automobile accident and now her parents are arguing all the time. The only place she feels at home is alone on the ocean in her dinghy, the *Titmouse*. When Koby frees a pilot whale tangled in a fishing net, the whales become her friends. But disaster strikes when Koby finds the whales stranded on a sand flat. All night long, Koby struggles to keep the whales and herself alive. When she and the whales are finally rescued, Koby proves to herself, her family, and to her classmates that she is special.

Through My Eyes by Ruby Bridges
Scholastic, 1999   GRADES 4–7

A highly visual autobiographical account of a brave young girl who became a national symbol when she integrated the New Orleans Public Schools. For an entire year, she was accompanied by U.S. marshals every day as she walked past screaming crowds of protestors to get to her first-grade classroom, in which she was the only student. Her memories are nicely supplemented with documentary photos and clippings from newspapers of the time, and with statements from her teacher and the educator Robert Coles.

Wringer by Jerry Spinelli
HarperCollins, 1997   GRADES 5+

Palmer dreads his tenth birthday. That's when all the boys become wringers, ones who wring the necks of injured pigeons that have been shot down during the town's annual Pigeon Day. Palmer keeps up the façade of being just like the other guys. He hangs out with Beans and Mutto and the rest of the gang, participating in the violence that surrounds their lives. Then one day, Palmer befriends a pigeon he calls "Nipper." When Nipper is in grave danger, Palmer must take action. This is a story about a boy who finds the courage to defy his friends' violence and struggles to save the life of an animal he has grown to love.

Zlata's Diary by Zlata Filipovic
Viking, 1994   GRADES 5+

Starting in September 1991, Zlata Filipovic chronicles her life during the upheaval and war in Sarajevo. Zlata's life is falling apart. As the sound of shelling constantly invades the air, Zlata tries to maintain a normal life without water, electricity, or heat. Fear intrudes on her thoughts as she practices her piano lessons to the cacophony of machine guns. *Zlata's Diary* depicts the life of a normal teenage girl thrown into the madness of war; death and destruction and sadness are not far behind.

13

Where Are
Your Survival Stories?

Climb or Die by Edward Myers
Hyperion, 1994 GRADES 5–8

In this survival story, Danielle and her brother Jake must use all of their athletic ability and ingenuity to scale Mount Remington in a snowstorm. Their parents have been badly injured in a car accident and the only help is at a weather station on top of the mountain. In order to get there, Danielle and Jake must put aside their sibling rivalries.

Danger along the Ohio by Patricia Willis
Clarion, 1997 GRADES 4–6

Amos, Clara, and Jonathan have come with their father to Ohio to seek a new life after their mother's death. On the way to Marietta, Indians ambush their riverboat, and the children are set adrift in the boat. They land, alone and afraid of further attacks from Indians, then set out on foot hoping to find their father.

Dave at Night by Gail Carson Levine
HarperCollins, 1997 GRADES 5–7

Dave cannot believe that his beloved papa has died and that his Uncle Jack will take only Gideon, Dave's brother, to live with him in Chicago. None of Dave's other relatives volunteer to take him in, so Dave's step-mother places him in the Hebrew Home for Boys. Dave must learn quickly how to survive in the HHB, how to keep the bullies from eating all his food, and how to steer clear of the abusive headmaster.

Far North by Will Hobbs
Avon, 1996   GRADES 6–9

Gabe and Raymond are traveling through British Columbia on a small
floatplane piloted by Gabe's friend Clint. Clint is so excited about flying
through this rugged, beautiful country that he can't resist the opportu-
nity to show the boys spectacular Virginia Falls. Their troubles begin
when the plane's engine won't restart and the current starts pulling the
plane toward the thundering falls. Can they keep the plane from going
over? What if they can't? How will they survive and be rescued?

A Girl Named Disaster by Nancy Farmer
Orchard, 1996   GRADES 5–8

Eleven-year-old Nhamo flees her village in Mozambique to avoid mar-
riage to a man she dislikes. She steals a boat and heads for Zimbabwe, the
homeland of her dead father. Along the way she must survive by her wits
in the wilderness and face many challenges, including hunger, wild animals, and the river itself.

Quake! by Joe Cottonwood
Scholastic, 1995   GRADES 5–8

Franny and Jennie's parents leave the girls at home to baby-sit Sidney,
Franny's younger brother, while they attend the World Series game in San
Francisco. Franny and Jennie haven't seen each other in a while and have
a lot of catching up to do. Soon though, their visit is interrupted by the
shakes and tremors that can only mean an earthquake has hit! Soon fires
start in their neighborhood and Mr. Vanda's cabin has slid down the hill.
Where can the girls go for help?

The Rescue of Josh McGuire by Ben Mikaelsen
Hyperion, 1991   GRADES 5–8

Things haven't been the same in Josh's family since his brother died in an
accident. When Josh's father kills a mother bear, Josh catches the cub and
brings it home. But when Josh learns that the cub will probably die at a
research laboratory he decides to run away. On his brother's motorcycle,
Josh heads to the mountains with Mud Flap, the family dog, and Pokey
the bear cub. Tension mounts when a bear attacks Mud Flap and Josh
wrecks the motorcycle. A week later, an injured Josh is found. But what
has become of Mud Flap and Pokey?

Stones in Water by Donna Jo Napoli
Dutton, 1997 GRADES 6–8

During World War II, Roberto and Samuele go to see an American cowboy movie at the local theater in Venice. German soldiers storm the building and take all the boys to a work camp where they must endure harsh conditions and live in fear that the soldiers may discover that Samuele is Jewish. The boys struggle to keep Samuele's secret while enduring near-starvation, freezing weather, and back-breaking work. Roberto escapes and joins the Italian resistance, sabotaging the war effort and helping to hide Jews.

Tracks in the Snow by Lucy Jane Bledsoe
Holiday House, 1997 GRADES 3–6

Erin can't get anyone to believe that Amy is missing and may be in trouble. After all, Amy is not always the most reliable baby-sitter. So Erin calls the police, but they are no help either. So Erin convinces her science project partner, Tiffany, to help her look for Amy. But while they are out in the woods, a spring blizzard hits. With no supplies or equipment, their rescue attempt turns into a struggle for their own survival.

White Water by P. J. Petersen
Simon & Schuster, 1997 GRADES 4–6

Greg's dad wants to go rafting on their next day out together. He thinks that Greg is too afraid of things and needs to face up to his fears. Greg does not want to go, but soon finds himself in an inflatable raft with his half-brother James and their dad. The cold river and rapid waters are frightening. When Greg's dad is bitten by a rattlesnake, will Greg brave the river to try to get him to help?

Winter Camp by Kirkpatrick Hill
Margaret K. McElderry, 1993 GRADES 4–6

See page 42 for a description of this book.

14

Do You Have
Any Books about Sports?

Centerfield Ballhawk by Matt Christopher
Illustrated by Ellen Beier   Little, Brown, 1992   GRADES 2–3

Nine-year-old José plays ball for the Peach Street Mudders. His buddies
say that José is the best fielder they have. And true enough, José makes
some great catches when he plays. But what he really wants to do is hit
.375 the way his dad did when he was in the minor league. Maybe then,
his dad will not be mad at him all the time. José tries practicing at the bat-
ting cage, reading up on techniques, and even splurges on a new bat.
Later he finds out that not everyone is born to be a hitter and that his dad
is just as proud that José is a great fielder.

Chicken Doesn't Skate by Gordon Korman
Scholastic, 1996   GRADES 5–8

Milo Neal decides that his science project this year will be, "The Complete
Life Cycle of a Link in the Food Chain." And the particular link he has in
mind is a chicken. When he brings the baby chick to science lab, Kelly
Marie names it Henrietta. Soon everyone wants to help with raising and
caring for Henrietta. Mrs. Baggio even builds a coop for her. When Zach
gets the job of babysitting Henrietta for the weekend, Adam ends up taking her to the hockey game and she becomes the school mascot. All this
fuss over a baby chicken! What will the class do when Milo wants to finish his project by turning Henrietta into a part of the human food chain?

Coaching Ms. Parker by Carla Heymsfeld
Illustrated by Jane O'Connor   Simon & Schuster, 1992   GRADES 3–5

Every year the Westbend Elementary sixth graders play a baseball game
against the teachers. This year, the new fourth-grade teacher, Ms. Parker,

is not very excited when she finds out she's needed on the team. She is terrible at baseball. Mike decides that he and his friends can help her out and make her better at baseball. But they have only two weeks! Can they teach their teacher?

Coco Grimes by Mary Stolz
HarperCollins, 1994 GRADES 3–5

Eleven-year-old Thomas lives with his grandfather in south Florida. They both love baseball and go to see as many spring training games each year as they can. This year they go to a game on Thomas's birthday, and Thomas almost catches a foul ball hit by his hero, Bobby Bonilla. Then, at his birthday party, Thomas receives a book about the Negro Baseball League. Thomas discovers that a former Negro League star lives in Miami, and he and his grandfather coax their old pickup into making the long trip to Miami.

Finding Buck McHenry by Alfred Slote
HarperCollins, 1991 GRADES 5–8

Jason knows a thing or two about baseball from collecting baseball cards. When Mr. Henry agrees to coach his flailing little league team, Jason is amazed at Mr. Henry's skills and knowledge about baseball. Jason becomes convinced that instead of just being the school custodian, Mr. Mack Henry is really the former star pitcher of the Negro Baseball League, Buck McHenry. Is Jason right?

Goalie by Susan Shreve
Tambourine, 1996 GRADES 4–6

After her mother's death, Julie takes on more and more of the responsibilities around the house. She cooks dinner and looks after her little sister. Then one day after school, Julie finds a note on the table. The note is from her dad, telling her that he's invited someone to have dinner with them. This "someone" just happens to be the mother of Julie's archrival on the soccer team. Could things be any worse?

Koufax Dilemma by Steven Schnur
Illustrated by Meryl Treatner Morrow, 1997 GRADES 4–6

Danny dreams of pitching in the major leagues someday, and his coach is going to let him pitch the season-opening game. His mother, however, has told him that he cannot play ball that night since it is the first night of Passover. Danny feels that this is very unfair, especially since another of his Jewish teammates will be playing. But Danny's mother reminds him that the great Sandy Koufax once missed a World Series game rather than play on a Jewish holiday. Can Danny find some way out of this dilemma?

Running Girl by Sharon Bell Mathis
Browndeer/Harcourt, Brace, 1997   GRADES 3–6

The first line eleven-year-old Ebonee Rose writes in her diary is "I AM A RUNNER!" As she trains for her next big race, her mind is filled with individual running statistics from all the female track stars she idolizes, and these she puts into her diary as well. She's also thinking about her biggest rival in her upcoming track event. Sharon Bell Mathis aptly captures the passion and near-obsession many young athletes have for their sport.

Season of Comebacks by Kathy Mackel
Illustrated by Scott Medlock   Putnam, 1997   GRADES 4–7

Molly Burrows' sister is the best softball pitcher in California. Molly finds it hard to live in Allison's shadow, especially when their dad spends most of his time coaching Allison and her team the Brookdale Blazers. Molly hates playing on the ten-year-olds' team, the Cookie Monsters, but an injury to the Blazers' catcher gives Molly a chance to move up. Can two rival sisters play on the same team?

Strong to the Hoop by John Coy
Illustrated by Leslie Jean-Bart   Lee & Low, 1999   GRADES K–3

Ten-year-old James knows he's too small to play four-on-four basketball with his older brother and his friends, so he's pleasantly surprised when he's asked to fill in at the last minute. Given the assignment to guard the biggest, toughest kid on the opposing team, James has his work cut out for him, but gets plenty of encouragement from one of his teammates. There's a lot of realistic action in this distinctive picture book illustrated with photo collages of real kids playing ball on an urban basketball court.

Taking Sides by Gary Soto
Harcourt, Brace, 1991   GRADES 4–7

It's hard enough for Lincoln Mendoza to leave his school and basketball teammates in a working-class Latino neighborhood when his family moves across town to a predominantly white middle-class neighborhood. It's even harder when he has to start all over again with a new team. But Lincoln faces his biggest challenge yet when he realizes that at his new school, he'll have to play against his old school team.

Trophy by Dean Hughes
Knopf, 1994   GRADES 4–6

Fifth-grader Danny is playing basketball for the first time this year. He practices hard and wants to play well, but he makes a lot of mistakes. More than anything, he wants to play well so that his dad will be proud of him. But his dad has other things on his mind, like drinking with his buddies at the shop where he's a mechanic and hitting the beers when he comes home from work. Sometimes Danny feels that his family might just explode.

Winning by C. S. Adler
Clarion, 1999   GRADES 5–8

Vicky loves playing tennis and wants desperately to make the eighth grade tennis team. Her practice and hard work pay off, but being on the team does not bring all the happiness she expects. First, she feels that her friendship with her best friend is at risk due to the increased amount of time she spends with the other players. Then, she discovers that her partner, Brenda, is so competitive that she expects Vicky to cheat in order to win. Just how important is winning to Vicky?

15

Do You Have
Any Mystery Books?

Cam Jansen and the Mystery at the Haunted House by David Adler
Illustrated by Susanna Natti   Viking, 1992   GRADES 2–4

Jennifer Jansen has a photographic memory, which is why she started being called "The Camera," or Cam for short. While spending the day at the amusement park, two teenage boys on skates bump into Aunt Katie. Later, Aunt Katie realizes that her wallet is missing. Could she have left her wallet at the entrance gate while paying for the tickets? Was it the teenage boys? Cam retraces their steps and finds something even scarier in the haunted house than the fake props.

The Case of the Goblin Pearls by Laurence Yep
HarperCollins, 1997   GRADES 5–7

In this first book in Yep's Chinatown Mystery series, twelve-year-old Lily Lew is excited about a visit from her glamorous movie-star aunt who's come to Chinatown to participate in the New Year parade. When some valuable pearls that were to be used in Aunt Lil's float suddenly disappear, she and young Lily work together to track the thieves and solve the mystery of the pearls' disappearance.

Case of the Desperate Drummer by E. W. Hildick
Macmillian, 1993   GRADES 3–5

The McGurk Organization's routine training exercise becomes real life when the group of detecting friends has to hide Mari's cousin, Yoshito Nakanishi, a world famous drummer, from two menacing looking men. Using their knowledge of concealing a vital witness, they hid Yoshito in a treehouse. But it isn't easy. First of all, they don't know why these men are

after Yoshito. And Yoshito uses anything he can get his hands on to practice his drumming, which irritates the neighbors.

Dead Letter: A Herculeah Jones Mystery by Betsy Byars
Viking, 1996   GRADES 3–5

Herculeah Jones and her friend Meat set out to find the woman who left
a message in the lining of a coat Herculeah bought at a second-hand
store. The message, stating that someone is going to kill the owner of the
coat, puts Herculeah on the trail of another case to solve. Is the owner of
the coat still alive or has she been murdered? As she puts her super sleuth
skills to work, Herculeah uncovers knowledge that someone wants to
remain secret. And that someone is willing to kill Herculeah to keep her
quiet. With the help of Meat and her parents, a police detective, and a private investigator, Heculeah solves the mystery of the woman and whose
coat she just had to buy.

Encyclopedia Brown and the Case of the Sleeping Dog by Donald
J. Sobol   Illustrated by Warren Chang   Delacorte, 1998   GRADES 3–4

Ten-year-old Encyclopedia Brown is at it again. Leroy Brown, better
known as Encyclopedia, is a voracious reader who never forgets what he's
read. The son of a police chief, Encyclopedia Brown is often asked by his
father to help solve mysteries. Among the many cases in this book,
Encyclopedia Brown solves the meaning of a secret message left by the
only person who knew the answer and happened to be stranded in Los
Angeles during an earthquake. He deals with bullies, sleeping dogs, missing fans, and stolen money. Solutions to the mysteries are in the back of
the book.

Face in the Bessledorf Funeral Parlor by Phyllis R. Naylor
Atheneum, 1993   GRADES 3–5

Bernie Magruder lives with his family in the Bessledorf Hotel. With help
from his friends Georgene and Weasel, Bernie investigates the strange
things that are happening at the Bessledorf Funeral Parlor, which happens to be right next door. Why did the owners of the funeral parlor build
a drive-in viewing window? Who is that person climbing up the fire
escape to the roof? And who stole the Higgins Roofing Company retire-
ment money? Bernie, Georgene, and Weasel aim to find out the answers
to these questions in this funny detective story.

Fire Bug Connection: An Ecological Mystery
by Jean Craighead George   HarperCollins, 1993   GRADES 4–6

Maggie spends every summer in the woods of Maine with her father, a botanist, and her mother, a dendrologist at the Biological Research Station. Unfortunately, she will not be the only kid around when Mitch, the son of a fellow scientist arrives. When Maggie receives a birthday gift of firebugs from a graduate student from the Czech Republic, she is thrilled. But something is going wrong. The firebugs are not growing up. They are "Peter Pans," staying in an immature state until they pop and die. With Mitch's help, Maggie finds the answer to this mystery and learns even more about nature, human and not so human.

Kidnap at the Catfish Café by Patricia Reilly Giff
Illustrated by Lynne Cravath   Viking, 1998   GRADES 2–4

Minnie lives with her older brother Orlando, a restaurant owner, in Sharkfin Bay. When purses are stolen from policewoman Kitty the Klutz and Mrs. Vorr, Minnie and her new cat Max set out to find the thief. At first, Minnie thinks it's the mysterious person that pushes her into the old clubhouse. Then she realizes that he is also after the thief. Surprises abound when both Max and the thief turn out to have hidden identities.

Nate the Great and Me by Marjorie Sharmat
Illustrated by Marc Simont   Delacorte, 1998   GRADES 1–3

When Nate the Great's friends celebrate "Detective Day" with Nate and his dog Sludge, they discover that someone is missing. Fang, Annie's dog, has run away. But why and where did he go? Fang was last seen being chased by two poodles and following a lady wearing fluffy bunny shoes. Nate the Great shares his detective skills with the reader in solving another mystery. Activities such as unscrambling a secret code, using invisible ink, and making pancakes and potato latkes are included in the back of the book.

Private I. Guana: The Case of the Missing Chameleon
by Nina Laden   Chronicle, 1995   GRADES K–3

When Private I. Guana learns of the disappearance of Leon, the chameleon, his first task is to make as many copies as possible of Leon's picture in different colors. He then sets out to find Leon, plastering the forest with posters and talking to lizards, turtles, and snakes. Then he spots the Lizard Lounge, a slimy place where reptiles hang out. On stage that night with Camille and the Gila Girls is a big surprise.

Sebastian (Super Sleuth) and the Copycat Crime by Mary Blount
Christian   Illustrated by Lisa McCue   Macmillan, 1993   GRADES 2–3

> Sebastian, a canine super sleuth, finds himself and his owner John at a mystery writers' conference helping guests solve a make-believe crime. But there is no time for play when a real crime is committed and John must solve the case by the end of the day. One manuscript is stolen in the morning, then another at lunch. As tempers rise and patience wanes, the writers accuse each other of jealousy and forgery. When John's bumbling attempts to solve the crime fail, it's Sebastian super sleuth to the rescue.

Something Wicked's in Those Woods by Marisa Montes
Harcourt, Brace, 2000   GRADES 5–7

> When Javi Cisneros and his little brother, Nico, move from Puerto Rico to California to live with their aunt after their parents' death, Javi notices strange goings-on in the woods behind their house. Is there any connection between what's happening out there and Nico's odd new imaginary friend? With the help of a neighbor girl, Willo, Javi begins to unravel a mystery connected to a long unresolved crime in the area.

Spider Kane and the Mystery at Jumbo Nightcrawler's by Mary
Pope Osborne   Illustrated by Victoria Chess   Knopf, 1993   GRADES 3–5

> In this sequel to *Spider Kane and the Mystery under the May-Apple*, Leon finds himself left out as the others in the group receive a special message from Spider Kane. But Spider Kane didn't send the message and Mimi, Hawk, Rosie, and La Mere are being held captive by Raymond Johnson, a notorious robberfly known as the Bald Buzzer. Raymond Johnson, along with his gang of hornets, thinks that Hawk stole gold from the United Ant Charities. And Raymond Johnson wants the gold. In the seedy world of Jumbo Nightcrawler's supper club, Spider Kane spins a plan to free the others and capture Raymond Johnson.

What's a Daring Detective Like Me Doing in the Doghouse?
by Linda Bailey   Illustrated by Pat Cupples
Albert Whitman, 1997   GRADES 3–5

> Stevie Diamond and Jesse Kulniki are neighbors and crime-solving partners. Their latest case involves the "Prankster," a person who steals underwear for the fun of it. The Prankster has now stolen the president's dog and Stevie and Jesse are hot on the trail. When Stevie gets a job with a dog-sitting service, she soon realizes that the stray found abandoned in the fenced yard at her workplace is the president's dog. But how did it get there? Now that she is in possession of the dog, how can Stevie explain to the police that she's not the Prankster?

16
Where Are Your "I Spy" or Other Search-and-Solve Books?

Alfred's Camera: A Collection of Picture Puzzles
by David Ellwand   Dutton, 1998   GRADES K–3

In the style of the "I Spy" books by Marzollo and Wick, this is a photo book with hidden objects. The point of the whole book is to find Alfred's missing camera, all the while finding other small hidden objects in the photos.

Do You See a Mouse? by Bernard Waber
Houghton Mifflin, 1995   GRADES K–3

Pictures and story reveal a small mouse living in a hotel right under staff noses. Detectives are called in to search the place, but still no one sees the mouse. Can you?

Haunted Castle: An Interactive Adventure Book by Leo Hartas
DK, 1997   GRADES 3–6

This mysterious puzzle book is somewhat more complicated than the average search-and-find book. There are symbols to find, codes to decode, doors to steer clear of, and captions that provide some direction to the reader. The pictures are vivid and there is much to see.

Hidden Pictures: Find a Feast of Camouflaged Creatures
by A. J. Wood   Illustrated by Nicki Palin   Millbrook, 1996   GRADES 1–5

The level of difficulty is rather high in this search-and-find book. Readers must have some knowledge of animals to pick them out of pictures. Each page has clues to what animals can be found.

Hide and Snake by Keith Baker
Harcourt, Brace, 1991   GRADES K–2

A snake winds its way through balls of yarn, shoelaces, socks, and the like. The observant onlooker will easily find the snake on each page.

I Spy Treasure Hunt: A Book of Picture Riddles Photos by
Walter Wick   Text by Jean Marzollo   Scholastic, 1999   GRADES K–5

Tiny objects hidden in photographs require a keen eye. This book's theme centers on objects usually found on or near a pirate ship. Even if children cannot find all the objects, they love looking at the pictures.

Look Alikes by Joan Steiner
Little, Brown, 1998   GRADES K–3

More than a thousand everyday objects are hidden in these photographs. A razor becomes a vacuum; an upside-down iron becomes a ship. The object of the book is to find specific objects mentioned on each page.

Puzzling Day in the Land of the Pharaohs by Scoular Anderson
Candlewick, 1995   GRADES 2–5

This search-and-find fits inside a story. There are dozens of objects to find and mazes to solve. The children in the stories must find their way through without any mishaps, and along the way the reader gets to help by finding the answers to the clues provided.

Riddle Road: Puzzles in Poems and Pictures by Elizabeth Spires
Illustrated by Erik Blegvad   Margaret K. McElderry, 1999   GRADES K–3

This book focuses more on the riddle, but the pictures hold the clues to the answer, which is revealed below, printed upside down.

When You're Not Looking: A Storytime Counting Book
by Maggie Kneen   Simon & Schuster, 1996   GRADES K–2

This counting book shows just one scene from a classic children's story. Each turn of the page increases the number of items to look for. The drawings are meant to be deeply investigated, and readers will also like the challenge of guessing which story the picture tells.

Where's Waldo? by Martin Handford
Candlewick, 1997   GRADES K–5

Waldo may have been the first breakthrough search-and-find series of the current era. Readers do nothing but search for Waldo. There is a small amount of reading involved on each page; the captions reveal what exact object readers should be on the lookout for.

17

Do You Have Any Really Scary Books?

The Boy with Dinosaur Hands: Nine Tales of the Real and Unreal
by Al Carusone   Illustrated by Elaine Clayton   Clarion, 1998   GRADES 4–7

This collection, by the author of *Don't Open the Door after the Sun Goes Down*, includes nine creepy horror stories that are short enough to read aloud. Some have a twist at the end and some are humorous.

Dark Thirty: Southern Tales of the Supernatural by Patricia McKissack   Illustrated by Brian Pinkney   Random, 1993   GRADES 5–8

Well-known author Patricia McKissack has written ten original stories based on African-American history that are both suspenseful and thought provoking. Brian Pinkney's scratchboard illustrations enhance every tale.

Ghost of a Hanged Man by Vivian Van Velde
Marshall Cavendish, 1998   GRADES 4–6

A curse from a hanged outlaw, a gypsy's fortune telling, and the Wild West all add up to a satisfyingly spooky adventure story. Ben's father, the sheriff, is one of the people that the outlaw Jake Barnett cursed before he died. A year after the hanging, strange things happen around town that make the townsfolk believe Jake's curse may be taking effect.

Ghosts, Vampires and Werewolves: Eerie Tales from Transylvania
by Mihai Spariosu and Dezso Benedek. Illustrated by Laszlo
Kubinyi   Orchard, 1994   GRADES 5–8

This collection of spooky stories from Transylvania has just enough gruesome details and surprise endings to keep readers involved to the very end. It also includes interesting background notes on where the stories come from and a good introduction.

Green Willow by Eileen Dunlop
Holiday House, 1993 GRADES 6–8

Kit, suffering from nightmares after the death of her sister, moves with her mother to an old house in Scotland. She meets Daniel, a 16-year-old struggling artist and together they discover a ghost in the old garden. As they uncover the story of the ghost, Kit begins to heal and friendships develop.

Haunted House: A Collection of Original Stories edited by
Jane Yolen and Martin H. Greenberg Illustrated by
Doron Ben-Ami HarperCollins, 1995 GRADES 3–6

Seven authors have written stories about 66 Brown's End, a home that seven different families have lived in over the years. A child in each family has discovered a different ghost in the house. The stories are suspenseful without being too scary, with a nice touch of humor added.

The Haunting of Holroyd Hill by Brenda Seabrooke
Puffin, 1995 GRADES 5–8

This is a ghost story and a love story with some Civil War history thrown in for good measure. Melinda and her family move back to Virginia where she and her brother Kevin and their new friend Dan discover not one, but two ghosts. As the children investigate the mystery, they learn of a secret from the Civil War that involves their family.

Please Do Not Touch: A Collection of Stories by Judith Gorog
Scholastic, 1993 GRADES 4–6

Those who enter the Pitu Gallery not only see with their eyes but also feel and hear the exhibits. The gallery has twelve rooms with twelve short stories, and when one enters the rooms, one experiences the stories firsthand.

Seven Spiders Spinning by Gregory McGuire
Illustrated by Dirk Zimmer Clarion, 1994 GRADES 3–5

Seven spiders, frozen since the ice age and sent to Harvard for study, are roaming the Vermont countryside as a result of a truck accident. The seven defrosted spiders huddle in the woods. Soon, a schoolgirl decides to take one home as a pet. One by one, the remaining six spiders set out to find their siblings. And one by one, the spiders meet their fate.

Seven Strange and Ghostly Tales by Brian Jacques
Philomel, 1991 Grades 4–6

Brian Jacques weaves seven strange tales into this collection of stories. In "The Lies of Henry Mawdsley," a boy's lies get the attention of the Devil himself. Henry is very proud of his lies. Unfortunately, those who know him also know he lies and do not believe his tales. But one day, Henry meets the Devil. If Henry signs a Soul Ownership Form H, zero, T, he will get everything he wants for a week. Then the Devil will take his soul. The deal is done, and the Devil comes back in a week to claim Henry's soul. But Henry is a world-class liar and even the Devil can be fooled.

Skull of Truth by Bruce Coville
Illustrated by Gary A. Lippincott   Harcourt, Brace, 1997   GRADES 3–5

Charlie has a problem. He can't stop telling lies. Until, that is, he finds Mr. Elives' magic shop and steals the skull of truth. Charlie is in an interesting predicament. The skull is lonely and talks incessantly and Charlie can't stop telling the truth. Truth, he learns, and telling the truth are not necessarily the same thing. Charlie learns a lesson or two about truth and friendship.

Sliver of Glass and Other Uncommon Tales by Anne Mazer
Illustrated by Broeck Stedman   Hyperion, 1996   GRADES 4–6

Containing eleven tales, this book features bizarre stories to chill the most warm-blooded animal. In one story, "The Golden Touch," M is obsessed with gold. One day he finds that everything he touches turns to gold. His son realizes what is happening and runs away, but unfortunately, M's wife and baby daughter turn into golden statues. M becomes thirsty and hungry, but everything he touches turns to gold. Then one day, M cries that he would do anything to lose the curse. So his golden touch disappears but no one believes him. He spends the rest of his life going from town to town searching for his son, surviving on handouts from a few good souls.

Terrifying Taste of Short & Shivery: Thirty Creepy Tales
retold by Robert D. San Souci   Illustrated by Lenny Wooden
Delacorte, 1998   GRADES 4–6

In this collection of thirty scary stories, San Souci covers the globe to bring chills and thrills. In "Yara-ma-yha-who," an Australian tale, two brothers often played and hunted together. This was good because they lived in the land of the Yara-ma-yha-who, little manlike creatures who captured lone hunters and ate them. One day the two brothers went hunting. One brother decided to rest by a fig tree. The other brother, afraid of the Yara-ma-yha-who, and called a coward by his brother, started for home. Soon, the disbelieving brother was eaten by the Yara-ma-yha-who and then turned into one of the manlike creatures.

Too Many Secrets by Betty Ren Wright
Scholastic, 1997   GRADES 4–7

Chad is hired to take care of Miss Beane's dog, Benson, when Miss Beane has to go to the hospital because she fell while investigating strange noises in her house. With the help of Baby, Miss Beane's parrot, Chad and his friend Jeannie try to find out who's making the noises.

Trespassers by Zilpha Keatley Snyder
Delacorte, 1995   GRADES 5–8

An abandoned mansion, a room full of wonderful toys, and a rumored ghost await Neely and her younger brother Grub when they sneak into Halcyon House. When the owners of the house return unexpectedly, Neely must protect her brother from an evil that lurks in the house.

Vampire Bugs: Stories Conjured from the Past by Sharon Dennis
Wyeth   Illustrated by Curtis E. James   Bantam, 1996   GRADES 4–6

Six scary stories feature conjure men, voodoo queens, and ghosts from African-American traditional stories, some of whom cast spells to trans-form children into bugs or birds. A nice blend of horror and humor.

Vengeance of a Witch-Finder by John Bellairs. Completed by
Brad Strickland   Illustrated by Edward Gorey   Dial, 1993   GRADES 4–6

It is 1951 and thirteen-year-old Sherlock Holmes fan Lewis Barnavelt and his uncle Jonathan are on vacation in Europe. While in England, they visit a distant cousin, Pelly Barnavelt. Lewis meets Bertie, the blind housekeeper's son, and the boys set out exploring. Curiosity gets the best of both boys when they loosen a brick to unleash demonic forces that were entombed by Lewis's ancestor in the 1600s. Lewis and Bertie must destroy the ghost of Malachiah Pruitt, a witch-finder with a demonic secret weapon of his own.

When the Chenoo Howls: Native American Tales of Terror by Joseph and
James Bruchac   llustrated by William Bock   Walker, 1998   GRADES 3–5

Twelve scary stories from the northeast woodland Indian traditions fea-ture native monsters such as the Flying Heads and the cannibal Keewah-kwee. Nine of the stories included here are traditional tales; three are original stories about legendary monsters; all are deliciously frightening.

18
What Are Some Good Ghost Stories?

Amber Cat by Hilary McKay
Illustrated by Gail Piazza   Margaret K. McElderry, 1997   GRADES 4–6

Robin Brogan has chicken pox and has to stay home from school. Then his best friend Dan catches them, and Robin's mother nurses the two boys back to health. But staying cooped up in a house all day long can be boring, even with the antics of neighbors Sun Dance Robinson and the rest of the Robinson family. When Robin's mother receives a letter from her childhood friend Charley, she is reminded of a time when she and her friends played with a mysterious girl named Harriet. But who or what was Harriet?

Face in the Mirror by Stephanie S. Tolan
Morrow, 1998   GRADES 5–9

Jared is to spend the summer in Michigan with his famous father, Phillip Kingsley, and his half brother, Tad. Phillip is producing a Star Wars version of Richard III and has promised Jared the role of the Prince of Wales. The biggest snags for Jared are that his half brother hates him and he knows nothing about the stage. He claims a space beneath the stage as his own and begins spending time with the ghost of actor Garrick Marsden. As Jared's relationship with Tad gets worse he begins plotting ways to get even. When Marsden offers him an option he takes it, and learns the truth about Marsden's past only just in time to prevent a tragedy.

Ghastly Gerty Swindle with the Ghosts of Hungryhouse Lane
by Sam McBratney   Illustrated by Lisa Thiesing
Henry Holt, 1993   GRADES 3–5

No one knows about Lady Cordelia, Sir James, and Bobbie except Miss Steadings and the Sweet children. When Miss Steadings advertises for a house companion, Gerty Moag answers the ad. But Gerty Moag is a swindler and with her son, Alexander the Grate, plans to steal Miss Steadings' antiques from right under her nose. When Miss Steadings invites the Sweet children to spend a couple of days with her in the country, Mr. and Mrs. Sweet could not be more ecstatic as they look forward to some peace and quiet. Gerty Moag, however, could not be more troubled. The children are getting in the way of her plans. Together with ghosts Cordelia, James, and Bobbie, the children investigate the missing antiques and put an end to Gerty and Alex's misdeeds.

Ghost Comes Calling by Betty Ren Wright
Scholastic, 1994   GRADES 3–5

Chad's dad buys a run-down cabin at the lake. When Chad's friend Jeanne tells him that a ghost haunts the cabin, Chad tries to ignore her comment. But when Chad sees the angry ghost for himself, he must find a way to set things right. He learns that the ghost, Tim Tapper, was wrongfully blamed for a truck accident involving children in the 1930s. Can Chad clear the name of Tim Tapper and end the frightening haunting of the cabin?

The Ghost Fox by Laurence Yep
Illustrated by Jean and Mou-sien Tseng   Scholastic, 1994   GRADES 3–5
See page 16 for a description of this book.

The Ghost of Grania O'Malley by Michael Morpurgo
Viking, 1996   GRADES 4–6
See page 44 for a description of this book.

Ghost of Popcorn Hill by Betty Ren Wright
Illustrated by Karen Ritz   Holiday House, 1993   GRADES 4–6

Martin and Peter want a great big dog when they go to the Humane Society to choose a pet. They come home with Rosie—not exactly as big a dog as they wanted, but the biggest their dad will let them have. The boys and their mom are especially glad to have Rosie around the house now that Martin has heard very scary laughter at night. But in spite of Rosie's presence, the boys still hear the scary "Ho-ho-ho" laughter at night in their bedroom. Can it be a ghost?

Ghoststalking by L. King Perez
Illustrated by Janet Hamlin   Carolrhoda, 1995   GRADES 4–6

Emilio's father has often threatened him that if he is not good la Llorona, the ghost woman who drowned her children a long time ago, will get him. When Emilio is at a loss as to what to do for his science project, his friend Chuy comes up with the idea of tracking la Llorona. Emilio's father is away in the fields, picking tomatoes, so Emilio and Chuy decide to hike into the mountains in order to find la Llorona. The boys take their sleeping bags and spend the night outside, waiting for the scream of la Llorona. When something does scream in the night, the boys are certain it is the ghost woman.

Graveyard Girl by Anna Myers
Walker, 1995   GRADES 4–6

It's 1878 and Eli's mother and little sister have died in a yellow fever epidemic that has hit the city of Memphis. Then his father deserts him and Eli is all alone. He accompanies his sister's casket to the cemetery where he meets Grace, the Graveyard Girl. Grace is the one who records the names of the dead and rings the bell for each yellow fever victim buried at Elmwood Cemetery. When Addie, an orphan, claims to have been told by her dead mother that the Graveyard Girl will help her, Eli is skeptical. Yet Eli finds himself taking care of Addie and eventually believing in Addie's mother's ghost. But what will happen when the Graveyard Girl becomes a victim of the deadly disease?

The Haunting of Holroyd Hill by Brenda Seabrooke
Puffin, 1995   GRADES 5–8

See page 61 for a description of this book.

Moaning Bones: African American Ghost Stories by Jim Haskins
Illustrated by Felicia Marshall   Lothrop, Lee & Shepard, 1998   GRADES 4–6

An outstanding collection of short ghost stories collected from African-American oral traditions, some dating back to slavery times, is well documented and nicely organized. The same author has issued an earlier collection of ghost stories, *The Headless Haunt* (HarperCollins, 1994).

Prietita and the Ghost Woman by Gloria Anzaldúa
Illustrated by Christina Gonzalez
Children's Book Press, 1996 GRADES 2–4

Brave Prietita goes into the woods to gather herbs for the *curandera* to help cure her mother's illness, even though her grandmother has warned her about la Llorona, the crying ghost woman of Mexican tradition. When she hears a woman crying in the woods, Prietita traces the sound and meets none other than la Llorona herself, who ends up offering a helping hand to the girl.

Taste of Smoke by Marion Dane Bauer
Clarion, 1993 GRADES 4–6

Thirteen-year-old Caitlin can't wait to go camping with her older sister Pam, whom she has not seen all year. Soon Caitlin's excitement turns to disappointment when Pam doesn't want to hear what Caitlin has to say and talks only about her life in college and her new boyfriend, Alex. When Alex shows up at the campsite, Caitlin is jealous and angry. In the woods, Caitlin meets Frank, a mysterious boy who thinks she is pretty. But something is not right, and Pam claims she cannot see Frank when Caitlin waves to him. With the help of Alex, Caitlin realizes that Frank is the ghost of a boy who died in the great Hinckley fire of 1894. But what does Frank want?

Time for Andrew by Mary Downing Hahn
Clarion, 1994 GRADES 4–6

Drew Tyler is spending the summer with his great-aunt in Missouri while his parents excavate a Roman dig in southern France. When Drew meets the ghost of Andrew, the great-great uncle for whom he is named, they agree to switch places. Drew goes back to 1910, and Andrew, dying of diphtheria, takes Drew's place in the present. Learning to live in 1910 is relatively easy for Drew as he copies the habits of Andrew's family. But Drew wants his own life back. Night after night, he and Andrew play marbles. If Drew wins, he can come back to the present.

19

I Want to Read
an Autobiography

The Abracadabra Kid: A Writer's Life by Sid Fleischman
Greenwillow, 1996   GRADES 4–7

Sid Fleischman didn't set out to be a writer. His first career was as a magician. How he went from magic tricks to children's novels is just part of his life story. The rest consists of his memories of childhood and adolescence, and details about his life as a writer. Filled with humor, each chapter cleverly opens with a question he has been asked in letters from young fans.

Leon's Story by Leon Walter Tillage
Farrar, Straus, & Giroux, 1997   GRADES 4–6

In this autobiography Leon, a sharecropper's son, relates his story of growing up in the South during the first half of the twentieth century. Leon was born in 1936 near Raleigh, North Carolina. The family, including his eight brothers and sisters, shared a house of five rooms that had no electricity or indoor plumbing. As Leon grew up, he witnessed the injustice done to people of color. His father was murdered, purposely run over by a car driven by young white boys. The Ku Klux Klan spewed hatred and fear among the people. Leon, however, knew that change must be brought about. As a high school student, he came in contact with Martin Luther King Jr. and participated in the nonviolent marches of the 1950s.

Looking Back: A Book of Memories by Lois Lowry
Houghton Mifflin, 1998   GRADES 4–7

Since both she and her father worked as professional photographers, Lois Lowry's personal photo album is quite a bit more artistic than most. Here she uses photos from her past to inspire memories about her life and to recall the inspiration she's had for many of her books for young people.

The Lost Garden by Laurence Yep   Messner, 1991   GRADES 4–7

As a Chinese-American kid growing up in San Francisco, Laurence Yep claims he often felt as though his life were a puzzle, and his mission was to find all the missing pieces. This metaphor serves as the focus of an outstanding autobiographical account by one of the most highly regarded authors for children and teens in the United States.

Seeing the Circle by Joseph Bruchac
Richard K. Owen, 1999   GRADES 2–4

"I was the kind of kid other kids didn't like," Bruchac confesses at the opening of his easy-to-read autobiography. He started out as a nerd and then developed into a star athlete. With both personas, people judged him by his outward appearance. He faced other challenges, too, as a child of mixed Native American and European heritage. One of the most revealing and heart-felt author autobiographies published to date.

Tallchief: America's Prima Ballerina by Maria Tallchief
with Rosemary Wells   Illustrated by Gary Kelley
Viking, 1999   GRADES K–3

From an early age, Maria Tallchief showed unusual talent for both music and dance. When Maria turned twelve and her parents suggested that she focus on developing just one of her gifts, she chose dance. Soon afterward, her family moved from an Osage Reservation to Los Angeles, so that she could train with some of the greatest ballet dancers of earlier generations. This unusual picture-book autobiography offers rare insight into the life of a woman completely devoted to her art.

Through My Eyes by Ruby Bridges
Scholastic, 1999   GRADES 4–7

See page 46 for a description of this book.

26 Fairmount Avenue by Tomie de Paola
Putnam, 1999   GRADES 2–4

This easy chapter book recounts what things were like in 1938 when Tomie was five years old. His family had just moved from an apartment to a house, he started school, and he recalls seeing the Disney movie *Snow White* on the big screen for the first time. An engaging glimpse into the childhood of well-known children's book artist.

Where the Flame Trees Bloom by Alma Flor Ada
Atheneum, 1994   GRADES 4–6

   Children's author Alma Flor Ada lived an idyllic life in an extended family as she was growing up in pre-Castro Cuba. In this entertaining autobiography, she introduces us to various family members from that period and re-creates several childhood events.

20

I Want to Read
a Biography

Anastasia's Album by Hugh Brewster
Hyperion, 1996   GRADES 3–5

Through photographs, drawings, pictures, and letters, we meet Anastasia, the fourth daughter of the Czar of Russia. Born on June 18, 1901, she lived a life of luxury as Her Imperial Highness the Grand Duchess Anastasia Nicholaievna. But her life of luxury was to end when the Russian Revolution began in 1917 and her family was taken prisoner by the new revolutionary government. Soon after her eighteenth birthday, Anastasia was murdered by the Bolsheviks along with the rest of her family.

At Her Majesty's Request: An African Princess in Victorian England by Walter Dean Myers   Scholastic, 1999   GRADES 4–7

Sarah Forbes Bonetta was born in the nineteenth century to one of the ruling families in West Africa. Orphaned at age five, she was brought to England, where Queen Victoria took a great interest in her and saw to it that she was brought up as a proper English gentlewoman. Walter Dean Myers uses excerpts from Sarah's letters and from Queen Victoria's journals to trace this young woman's fascinating life story.

Babe Didrikson Zaharias: The Making of a Champion
by Russell Freedman   Clarion, 1999   GRADES 5–8

One of the greatest athletes of the twentieth century is brought to life in this in-depth but highly readable biography. Young Babe demonstrated her athletic prowess at an early age, but throughout her life had to face both gender and class discrimination in order to rise to the top in sports such as track and field, basketball, and golf. Witty, self-confident, and outspoken, Babe was a true character from start to finish.

Crazy Horse by Judith St. George
Putnam, 1994   GRADES 5–8

The famous Oglala warrior Tashunka Witko, popularly known as Crazy Horse, led his people in battle many times in the nineteenth century and has gone down in history as one of the great military minds of modern times. There have been many conflicting reports on his life; these are pulled together by an author who did extensive primary research in Nebraska and South Dakota to create a compelling biography of a complex man.

Dragon Bones and Dinosaur Eggs: A Photobiography
of Roy Chapman Andrews by Ann Bausum
National Geographic Society, 2000   GRADES 3–7

From the time he was a boy in Wisconsin, Roy Chapman Andrews was fascinated with the natural world and, as a young man, he managed to get a janitorial job at the American Museum of Natural History, just to be close to the type of work to which he aspired. He quickly rose through the ranks and eventually led scientific expeditions to unexplored lands, including remote areas of Mongolia where he discovered dinosaur fossils. Andrews' adventurous spirit and robust style of life have led many to believe that he was the inspiration for the movie hero Indiana Jones.

First in the Field: Baseball Hero Jackie Robinson
by Derek T. Dingle   Hyperion, 1998   GRADES 3–5

Robinson had many qualities that led to his selection as the first African-American baseball player in the major leagues, not the least of which was his formidable athletic talent. In college sports, he excelled not just in baseball, but in basketball, football, and track, and in his years in the Negro Leagues he played against such greats as Cool Papa Bell, Satchel Paige, and Josh Gibson. While serving in the U.S. military during World War II, Robinson demonstrated a commitment to social justice that served him well as he faced the obstacles presented to him in the major leagues.

Sky Pioneer: A Photobiography of Amelia Earhart
by Corinne Szabo   National Geographic Society, 1997   GRADES 3–7

Numerous documentary photographs accompany this excellent account of the life of the great aviator who broke down many social barriers in her short lifetime. The text emphasizes Earhart's many accomplishments in the air and her record-breaking flights, rather than dwelling on the mystery of her disappearance.

Spellbinder: The Life of Harry Houdini by Tom Lalicki
Holiday House, 2000   GRADES 4–7

Born in Budapest, Hungary, in 1874, Erich Weiss came to America as a young child when his father took a position as rabbi in Appleton, Wisconsin. From an early age, Erich helped earn money for his family by performing magic acts and, when he had perfected his art, he took the stage name Harry Houdini. He soon became known throughout the world for his uncanny ability to escape from any prison cell, straitjacket, locked box, or, most famously, what was called the Chinese water-torture cell.

Toussaint L'Ouverture: The Fight for Haiti's Freedom
by Walter Dean Myers   Illustrated by Jacob Lawrence
Simon & Schuster, 1996   GRADES 3–5

François Dominique Toussaint was born in Haiti in 1743, the son of an African who taught François to read and speak French. Toussaint grew up to work as a coachman on a plantation. He had heard about the American Revolution and hoped that one day he would be free. In 1791, the blacks on the island rebelled against the plantation owners. Toussaint joined the rebellion and soon became a leader. Eventually, Toussaint laid down his arms thinking that blacks would be free. But he was taken to a prison in France where he died in 1803. His efforts were not in vain, however, as Haiti became a country in 1804.

Wilma Mankiller by Linda Lowery
Illustrated by Janice Lee Porter   Carolrhoda, 1996   GRADES 3–5

A highly accessible biography outlines the life of the first woman Chief of the Cherokee Nation. Throughout her life, Wilma Mankiller has had to endure both racism and sexism, but she never stopped believing in herself or lost sight of her commitment to help other people.

21

Do You Have Any
Picture-Book Biographies?

Duke Ellington by Andrea Davis Pinkney
Illustrated by Brian Pinkney   Hyperion, 1997   GRADES K–3

Born April 29, 1899, Edward Kennedy "Duke" Ellington grew up in
Washington, D.C. When his parents enrolled him in piano lessons, Duke
was bored. He would have rather played baseball than learn the piano.
But one day, Duke heard someone playing ragtime. He found himself
back at the piano trying to play his own ragtime tunes. With more and
more practice, Duke soon became a hit at parties, pool halls, country
clubs and cabarets. Next, Duke formed his own band and left
Washington, D.C. for Harlem. In 1927, Duke performed at the Cotton
Club and his music was broadcast live over the radio. Duke Ellington
became a household name. Duke Ellington died in 1974, but his influ-
ence on music is alive still.

Eleanor by Barbara Cooney
Viking, 1996   GRADES K–3

When Eleanor Roosevelt was born in 1884, her mother was disappointed
because she was neither a boy nor a beautiful baby. Eleanor was a shy
child and clung to her nanny, who spoke to her only in French. Eleanor
adored her absent father but her mother called her Granny because she
was old fashioned and funny looking. Eleanor's family was wealthy but
that did not keep her from seeing poverty. One year, she and her father
helped serve Thanksgiving dinner to poor newsboys. Eleanor and her
brothers went to live with their grandmother after their parents died. Life
with Grandma Hall was a challenge, as Eleanor still felt like an outsider.
At age fifteen, Eleanor was sent to boarding school in England where she

blossomed and became her own woman. This retelling of Eleanor's childhood includes an author's note regarding her accomplishments as an adult.

Joan of Arc by Diane Stanley
Morrow, 1998   GRADES 4–6

Joan of Arc was born in the village of Domremy in France in 1412. Although, like most peasants, she could not read or write, Joan was a pious girl who said her prayers faithfully. When Joan was about thirteen, she saw a vision of the Archangel Michael. As Joan grew older, her visions told her that God had a mission for her. Later, Joan dressed as a man and went into battle to save the city of Orleans from the English. Declared a heretic, Joan was burned at the stake in 1431. In 1920, the Roman Catholic Church declared Joan a saint.

Malcolm X: A Fire Burning Brightly by Walter Dean Myers
Illustrated by Leonard Jenkins   HarperCollins, 2000   GRADES 3–7

For reluctant readers or for those who want a brief overview of Malcolm X's life, this excellent biography focuses on the turning points in his life. Each double-page spread includes a well-chosen quotation from *The Autobiography of Malcolm X* as well as concise text that recounts major events. Concludes with a chronology.

Minty: A Story of Young Harriet Tubman by Alan Schroeder
Illustrated by Jerry Pinkney   Dial, 1996   GRADES K–3

This story is a fictionalized account of the early life of Harriet Tubman, a slave on the Brodas plantation in Maryland in the 1820s. Minty was known as a "difficult slave." She dreamed of escaping the harsh life on the plantation so her father showed her how to read the stars and the trees and taught her to swim. In real life, Minty did escape. At twenty-four and married to a free man, John Tubman, Minty made her way to Philadelphia. But she was not through. She made the dangerous journey back to Maryland many times to help hundreds of slaves escape. The route of escape was called the Underground Railroad and Minty knew it well.

My Name Is Georgia: A Portrait by Jeanette Winter
Harcourt, Brace, 1998   GRADES K–3

Georgia O'Keeffe was born in Wisconsin in 1887. She had always known what she wanted, and at the age of twelve she knew that she wanted to be an artist. She went to school in Chicago and drew. She went to school in New York City and painted. She went to the Texas plains and brought her paintings back to New York City. She painted things BIG so people would notice them. But still she felt something was missing. Georgia moved to New Mexico, where she painted the desert and mountains. Georgia O'Keeffe lived to be ninety-eight years old.

Purple Mountain Majesties: The Story of Katherine Lee Bates and "America the Beautiful" by Barbara Younger
Illustrated by Stacey Schuett   Dutton, 1998   GRADES K–3

She may not be a household name, but the poem she penned in 1893 is certainly well-known across the nation. The story of how an adventurous young school teacher came to write "America the Beautiful" during a cross-country trip to climb Pike's Peak is as interesting as any work of fiction. An immediate hit when it was published two years later in a magazine, her poem spurred a national contest for the right tune. Over nine hundred entries were rejected in favor of "God Save the King," the tune still being used for the poem today.

Snowflake Bentley by Jacqueline Briggs Martin
Illustrated by Mary Azarian   Houghton Mifflin, 1998   GRADES K–3

Willie Bentley devoted his life to a study of snowflakes, perfecting photographic techniques that would capture a snowflake's image before it melted away. Martin's intriguing portrait of this unusual, slightly eccentric character who wanted others to appreciate the beauty of snowflakes is accompanied by distinguished woodcut illustrations by Mary Azarian.

Starry Messenger by Peter Sís
Farrar, Straus, & Giroux, 1996   GRADES 3–5

Galileo Galilei was born February 15, 1564, in the city of Pisa, Italy. As a professor of mathematics, Galileo did many experiments, even proving Aristotle wrong. Galileo then built a telescope and published his findings in a book called *The Starry Messenger*. But Galileo's findings were considered heretical by the Church and he was condemned to spend the rest of his life locked in his house. Galileo's findings were proven right and he was eventually pardoned by the Church over three hundred years later.

Wilma Unlimited by Kathleen Krull
Illustrated by David Diaz   Harcourt, Brace, 1996   GRADES K–3

Wilma Rudolph was born in Clarksville, Tennessee, in 1940, weighing just over four pounds at birth. Her mother already had nineteen children so Wilma was never left alone. Although sickly as a child, Wilma ran instead of walking and jumped instead of hopping. But at the age of five, she caught both scarlet fever and polio. She survived, but the polio left her crippled. Then one day in church, Wilma removed the brace and walked on her own. Soon she was playing basketball and running. Wilma made history by winning three gold medals in the Rome Olympics in 1960. Her determination and courage made her a household name.

22

I Want to Read
Some Realistic Fiction

Amber Brown Is Feeling Blue by Paula Danziger
Illustrated by Tony Ross   Putnam, 1998   GRADES 3–5

> Amber Brown has to make a choice. Should she go to Walla Walla, Washington, with her mom and her mom's boyfriend for Thanksgiving or stay home with her dad? Amber's dad is moving back from Paris, France, and wants to spend some time with her. Unfortunately, Amber has told her mother that she would love to go to Walla Walla. And to top it all off, the new girl in class is named Kelly Green. All of a sudden, Amber's happy world is shadowed by insecurity.

Blue Sky, Butterfly by Jean Van Leeuwen
Dial, 1996   GRADES 3–5

> Twig's life is ruined. Her father has left, her mother is listless, and her brother just sits in his room and strums his guitar. Every day, Twig attempts to adjust to the emptiness in her life. Her mother's inability to function leaves Twig trying to maintain a sense of normalcy, but things get worse rather than better. Finally, Twig calls the only hope she has, her world-traveling Grandma Ruthie.

Flip-Flop Girl by Katherine Paterson
Dutton, 1994   GRADES 4–6

> Vinnie's father has just died and now her mother is moving Vinnie and her little brother in with her father's stepmother. No one pays any attention to Vinnie, just to her little brother Mason, who stopped talking when their father died. Vinnie's life has been turned upside down and inside

out. Her father would understand but he is not here anymore. She feels all alone until she meets the "flip-flop" girl.

The Friends by Kazumi Yumoto. Translated by Cathy Hirano
Farrar, Straus, & Giroux, 1996 GRADES 5–7

Sixth-graders Kiyama, Kiwabe, and Yamashita begin to spy on a reclusive old man in their neighborhood in an attempt to satisfy their curiosity about death. But under their watchful eyes, the old man undergoes a transformation—instead of dying, he seems to have developed a renewed interest in life. The realistic intergenerational friendship that develops between the boys and the old man is set against the backdrop of contemporary Tokyo, where the boys are preparing for an end-of-term exam that will determine the directions their lives will take.

Ginger Brown: Too Many Houses by Sharon Wyeth
Illustrated by Cornelius Wright   Random, 1996 GRADES 1–2

Ginger's parents are getting a divorce and Ginger has to stay first with her mom's parents then with her dad's parents during the summer while her mother works. Ginger's mom's parents live in an apartment building and teach her how to make pies. Ginger's dad's parents live on a farm and teach her how to swim and collect eggs.

Heart of a Chief by Joseph Bruchac
Dial, 1998 GRADES 5–8

As he enters middle school, eleven-year-old Chris, a member of the Penacook tribe, must confront some issues that are realities for contemporary Native Americans, including alcoholism, casino gambling, and school sports teams that use Indian mascots. Chris faces some tough challenges and stereotypes but finds that he's equal to the task.

In-Between Days by Eve Bunting
Illustrated by Alexander Pertzoff   HarperCollins, 1994 GRADES 3–6

After his mother's death, it was just George, his brother James and their dad and George wants to keep it that way. But now his father is seeing Caroline, a woman who threatens to disrupt George's life on little Dove Island. George finds a way to get Caroline off the island and out of his life. But something is wrong. He misses Caroline too. George finally understands that Caroline will never replace his mom and that there is room in their family for another.

Joey Pigza Swallowed the Key by Jack Gantos
Farrar, Straus & Giroux, 1998   GRADES 4–6

Joey is wound up. His spring is wound so tight that sometimes even his medication for attention deficit disorder doesn't help. Joey can't sit still; his mind and body are constantly racing, much to the consternation of his mother, teacher, and classmates. According to his grandmother, Joey is just like his father, who left home when Joey was in kindergarten. His mother left shortly afterwards, leaving Joey with a grandmother who threatened to put him in the refrigerator if he didn't behave. Now that his mother has returned, the long hard journey to recovery, amidst episodes of key-swallowing and injury to classmates, can begin for both Joey and his mom.

Junebug by Alice Mead
Farrar, Straus & Giroux, 1995   GRADES 3–5

Reeve McClain Jr., also known as Junebug, lives in the projects amid drugs and violence. He has to take care of his little sister Tasha while his mother is at work, and that gives him an excuse to stay away from the streets. He dreads turning ten, when he will be expected to hang out with the big kids, run some errands, and make some money. Unlike most kids in the projects, Junebug's favorite thing to do is to collect bottles. Into the bottles he slips little pieces of paper with wishes. His birthday wish is to float his bottle collection like a flotilla, in the hope that someone will find one and make his wish come true.

Just Juice by Karen Hesse
Illustrated by Robert Andrew Parker   Scholastic, 1998   GRADES 3–5

Nine-year-old Juice just isn't one for schooling. Letters are hard for her to read. Besides, her job is to comfort Pa who once again has lost his job. As her two older sisters head off for school and her two younger sisters stay home with a pregnant Ma, Pa shares a secret with Juice. It's an official looking letter that neither of them can read. With the help of Malarkey, Juice's older sister, they find out that they will lose their inherited property if they don't pay the overdue taxes. And to top it all off, the truant officer puts his foot down about Juice's reluctance to go to school.

Maybe Yes, Maybe No, Maybe Maybe by Susan Patron
Illustrated by Dorothy Donahue   Orchard, 1993   GRADES 3–4

As the middle child, PK is stuck between two sisters. If that weren't bad enough, her older almost-teenager sister, Megan, is "gifted" and has to be left alone. On the other hand, Rabbit, her younger sister, is a nonstop quizzer. To top it all off, PK's family is moving to a new apartment. What will she do with all her collectibles? How can she tell Rabbit stories without the built-in laundry hamper? After moving, PK decides to visit her old apartment and realizes the fact that some things change doesn't mean that other things can't stay the same.

Mick Harte Was Here by Barbara Park
Knopf, 1995   GRADES 4–6

Barbara Park writes about death and denial through the eyes of Phoebe, a thirteen-year-old girl who has just lost her brother in a bicycle accident. Right from the start, Phoebe lets everyone know that her brother Mick has died. In Phoebe's narrative, we learn that funny, prankster Mick was not only close to her in age but close to her heart. She misses Mick, but how can she make sure he does not become just a memory?

Missing May by Cynthia Rylant
Orchard, 1992   GRADES 4–6

Life without the sweet touch of May just isn't the same. No one grieves the loss of May more than Ob, not even Summer. When orphaned Summer came into their lives, she learned the meaning of true love through May and Ob. Now May is gone and Ob is listless. Then Cletus, a classmate of Summer's, starts hanging around. Ob perks up and shows real interest in what Cletus has to say. Together the three of them conspire to reach May through a spiritualist. When their plans fail, they find a simple yet profound way to connect to May after all.

My Name Is Brain Brian by Jeanne Betancourt
Scholastic, 1993   GRADES 3–5

Brian wants to be cool and hang out with his friends in the Jokers club. They hate school and they hate the thought of starting sixth grade. Brian's year doesn't start off right. He stumbles while reading aloud to the class and his spelling is atrocious. Luckily, his new sixth-grade teacher recognizes Brian's problem: he's dyslexic. As Brian learns new ways to cope with dyslexia, he sees his friends in a new light and learns the true meaning of friendship.

P.S. Longer Letter Later by Paula Danziger and Ann M. Martin
Scholastic, 1998   GRADES 4–6

Twelve-year-olds Tara*Starr and Elizabeth are totally different and are best friends. When Tara*Starr moves away, the girls continue their friendship through letters. In their letters, the girls express joy, anger, jealousy, and love about those around them and to each other. Elizabeth is worried about her parents. Her dad is coming home from work later and later. Are they getting a divorce? And is Tara*Starr making new friends and forgetting about Elizabeth? Tara*Starr is worried about her parents. They are becoming so normal. Are they planning to have another child? On their rocky road to understanding life, both girls realize that change isn't necessarily all bad.

Strider by Beverly Cleary
Illustrated by Paul O. Zelinsky   Morrow, 1991   GRADES 4–6

In this sequel to *Dear Mr. Henshaw,* Leigh Botts is fourteen and writing in his diary again. This time, Leigh and his friend Barry come across a stray dog. When it is evident that the dog, named Strider, has been abandoned, Leigh and Barry decide to own him jointly. The bond between Strider and Leigh grows stronger when Barry spends a month at his mother's house in Los Angeles. Strider not only gives Leigh companionship, but helps him to cope with the struggles in his life. Leigh desperately wants Strider as his own. Through episodes of acceptance and alienation, Leigh realizes that human friendships are just as important.

Sun and Spoon by Kevin Henkes
Greenwillow, 1997   GRADES 4–6

Ten-year-old Spoon Gilmore misses Gram, his deceased grandmother. Gram has only been dead for two months, yet Spoon is afraid that he is going to forget her. With much thought, Spoon steals the deck of cards that Gram used when Spoon, Gram, and Pa played triple solitaire together. Having Gram's cards makes Spoon feel somehow closer to her. But Spoon doesn't realize how much Pa misses her too; every night, Pa would take out Gram's cards and play solitaire. Now the cards are missing and Pa isn't acting the same. Spoon's conscience won't let him keep the cards, but what will replace them?

What Jamie Saw by Carolyn Coman
Front Street, 1995   GRADES 5–7

What Jamie saw was Van, his mom's boyfriend, throwing his little sister Nin across the room. She was being thrown like a rocket and there was nothing Jamie could do but watch. Luckily, his mom caught her just in time. Immediately, Jamie's mom puts the children in the car and leaves. They leave Van to squeeze out an existence in a tiny bullet-shaped trailer.

Yolonda's Genius by Carol Fenner
Margaret K. McElderry, 1995   GRADES 4–6

Yolonda is a big girl for her age, smart and sassy. Her little brother Andrew, by comparison, is small for his age and streetwise Yolonda must protect him. Yolonda's mother, a widow, moves the family to a small town in order to get away from the crime and drugs of Chicago. But Yolonda soon finds out that drugs and crime are everywhere and takes on the bullies that harass Andrew, much to the delight and admiration of her classmates. Never one to talk much, Andrew uses his mouth organ instead of his talking voice. Only Yolonda knows what a genius Andrew is, and she sets out to prove it.

23

Where Are Your Historical Fiction Books?

(Picture Books)

Across the Wide Dark Sea: The Mayflower Journey by Jean Van Leeuwen
Illustrated by Thomas B. Allen   Dial, 1995   GRADES K–3

> In 1620, a group of people, including thirty children, crossed the Atlantic Ocean to find freedom of worship in a new land. A boy recounts the story of his family's long hard journey of boredom, sickness, and danger. After nine long weeks, the group finally reaches shore, naming their newfound land Plymouth Plantation. Sickness and the harshness of winter threaten their security, but they must build houses and plant crops in order to survive. When they survive the winter, hope is in their hearts.

Amistad Rising: A Story of Freedom by Veronica Chambers
Illustrated by Paul Lee   Harcourt, Brace, 1998   GRADES 4–6

> When slave merchants in West Africa kidnap Cinque, he thinks he will never see his wife and children again. Bound by iron shackles, Cinque and over five hundred other Africans are imprisoned on a ship headed for Cuba. When the ship arrives in Cuba, Cinque is transferred to another ship, the *Amistad.* On the *Amistad,* Cinque finds a way to overthrow the crew. Lost and wanting to go back to Africa, Cinque eventually lands in Connecticut, where his group is tried for mutiny. With the help of John Quincy Adams, Cinque becomes a free man once more.

Annushka's Voyage by Edith Tarbescu
Illustrated by Lydia Dabcovich   Clarion, 1998   GRADES K–3

> After waiting a year, Annushka and her little sister Tanya are on the way from a small Russian village to New York at the beginning of the twentieth century. Their father immigrated to America a year before and the girls are plagued with mixed feelings of sadness and excitement as they

leave their grandparents in Russia for the voyage to see their father again. Annushka and Tanya arrive at Ellis Island, where they are processed as immigrants. Holding their grandmother's candlesticks high, the girls find their father and a new home.

Bracelet by Yoshiko Uchida
Illustrated by Joanna Yardley   Philomel, 1993   GRADES K–3

It's 1944 and Japanese Americans are being sent to prison camps in remote areas of the United States. Emi, a Japanese-American girl, must leave her best friend Laurie, her home, and most of her possessions. When Laurie gives Emi a bracelet as a going-away present, Emi swears that she will cherish it forever. Emi and her family are taken on a bus to an abandoned racetrack where they must live in old horse stalls. When Emi loses her bracelet, she is devastated. Then she realizes that she doesn't need a bracelet to remember those things that are in her heart.

Drummer Boy: Marching to the Civil War by Ann Turner
Illustrated by Mark Hess   HarperCollins, 1998   GRADES 2–5

A young boy lies about his age and joins the Civil War, becoming a drummer boy. He leaves a note for his Pa, bundles up his clothes, and climbs out the window to sign up. His first battle is the worst as bullets whizz past him and men die before his eyes. He soon learns that beating his drum drowns out the sounds of crying and dying and makes the men feel brave.

Encounter by Jane Yolen
Illustrated by David Shannon   Harcourt, Brace, 1992   GRADES K–3

When a young Taino boy sees Columbus's men land on the island of San Salvador, he warns the villagers to stay away from them. But the people of pale color fascinate the villagers. Columbus's men are deeply interested in the gold armbands and gold rings the islanders are wearing. The boy is chosen to go on the big canoe with the visitors and realizes he is going farther and farther from land. He silently slips out of the canoe and warns everyone he can about the pale strangers.

Mirette on the High Wire by Emily McCully
Putnam, 1992   GRADES K–3

A young girl named Mirette lives with her mother in the Paris of a hundred years ago. Mirette's mother runs a boardinghouse that is popular with traveling players from all over the world. When a tightrope walker arrives at the boardinghouse, Mirette is fascinated by his feats and soon becomes a pupil of Bellini the great. Unfortunately, Bellini has become afraid to walk the tightrope himself anymore. With Mirette's encouragement, he faces up to his fear.

Moonstick: The Seasons of the Sioux by Eve Bunting
Illustrated by John Sandford   Joanna Cotler, 1997   GRADES K–3

A young Dakota boy describes the changes of the year according to the thirteen moons of the Sioux year. Starting in the spring with the moon of the birth of calves, the boy's father cuts a moon-counting stick. Daily life continues under the strawberry moon as his mother and sisters make leggings and moccasins. During the cherry-ripening moon, the men dance and hunt. As the seasons and moons pass, the ground is covered in white. When the snows melt and the thirteenth moon dies, it's time to cut another stick.

Nim and the War Effort by Milly Lee
Illustrated by Yangsook Choi   Frances Foster, 1997   GRADES K–3

Nim, a Chinese girl living in San Francisco's Chinatown, is determined to collect the most papers for her school during the war effort of World War II. Her elementary school is having a paper drive to see who can collect the most newspapers. Finding a warehouse full of papers is a blessing to Nim—until she realizes that she has disgraced her family. With the help of her grandfather, Nim accepts her triumph graciously and learns what it means to be an American.

Pink and Say by Patricia Polacco
Philomel, 1994   GRADES 4–6

The author tells the story of her great-great-grandfather Say, who was befriended by a young black soldier in the Union Army during the Civil War. Sheldon Russell Curtis, also known as Say, has been left for dead in a field in Georgia. A black soldier, Pinkus Aylee, known as Pink, rescues him. Now, both boys are in danger of being caught by marauders. Pink takes Say home with him, putting his mother's life in danger. The youths' friendship grows, but they are captured and taken to Andersonville prison.

Redcoats and Petticoats by Katherine Kirkpatrick
Illustrated by Ronald Himler   Holiday House, 1999   GRADES 2–4

When Redcoats take over their home, Thomas Strong's family moves to a little cottage on the water. His father has been arrested as a traitor and taken to a prison ship in New York Harbor. Each day, Thomas' mother sends him out in his rowboat to watch for whaleboats and asks him what he has seen. Then she hangs red or black petticoats on the clothesline. Thomas soon learns that he is helping his mother spy on the Redcoats. The color of the petticoats indicates where the Redcoats and whaleboats are hiding. Thomas and his mother are eventually able to free his father.

Sweet Clara and the Freedom Quilt by Deborah Hopkinson
Illustrated by James Ransome   Knopf, 1993   GRADES K–5

Sweet Clara, a slave, is sent to work in the Big House when she proves that she can sew tiny stitches. Working in the Big House is a lot different from working in the fields, and soon Sweet Clara is able to piece together in her mind a map to freedom. Using leftover scraps from her sewing, Sweet Clara sews a quilt using blues for rivers and lakes and greens for fields. Her quilt becomes a map to freedom along the Underground Railroad. Leaving her quilt behind for others to follow, Sweet Clara escapes with Young Joe to freedom, following the North Star to Canada.

The Wagon by Tony Johnston
Illustrated by James Ransome   Tambourine, 1996   GRADES 2–4

A young boy describes his life as a slave. While helping his Papa build a wagon for the owner, the boy longs to have the wagon for himself. The master put his Papa in charge of the wagon to get supplies, sometimes even slaves. As his resentment builds, the boy takes an axe to the wagon wheels. Then he hears his grandmother talk about how Mr. Lincoln chopped wood to help himself get on in life. When the war is over and the family is freed, they are given the wagon and two mules so they can start a new life. Upon hearing of the death of President Lincoln, the boy, free to go where he pleases, wants to go to the funeral.

24

Where Are Your
Historical Fiction Books?
(Eighteenth Century and Earlier)

African Mask by Janet E. Rupert
Clarion, 1994   GRADES 5–8

   In eleventh-century Yoruba, twelve-year-old Layo lives with her family of
   potters. She wants to be a potter like her grandmother but she knows it's
   not up to her to choose her husband or the type of household she will be
   living in. When she accompanies her grandmother to the city of Ife, Layo
   meets and instantly dislikes her betrothed. Soon she realizes that things
   are not as they seem and she learns from her grandmother more than just
   the art of pottery. Glossary and pronunciation guide included.

Beaded Moccasins: The Story of Mary Campbell
by Lynda Durrant   Clarion, 1998   GRADES 5–9

   A fictionalized account of twelve-year-old Mary Campbell, kidnapped by
   Indians in 1759. When Mary is kidnapped by a group of Delaware, she is
   forced to travel away from her homestead in Pennsylvania to the Ohio
   wilderness. Taken from her family to replace a dead Delaware girl, Mary
   soon learns the way of the Delaware. As thoughts of escape slowly die
   with each year, Mary begins to love and depend on her new family. When
   the tribes' garden is flooded, Mary saves the corn by digging trenches
   around the crop and is renamed Woman Who Saved the Corn. Glossary
   of words and names included.

Captive by Joyce Hansen
Scholastic, 1994   GRADES 4–6

   See page 43 for a description of this book.

Catherine, Called Birdy by Karen Cushman
Clarion, 1994   GRADES 6–10

This Newbery Honor Book, set during the Middle Ages, is the journal of fourteen-year-old Catherine. Catherine, or Birdy as she is called, finds the life of a young woman tedious with all the sewing and cooking and other chores. As her father tries to find a suitable husband for her, Catherine, who is witty and intelligent, finds ways to scare off several of them.

Children of the Longhouse by Joseph Bruchac
Dial, 1996   GRADES 3–6

Eleven-year-old twins Ohkwa'ri and Otsi:stia live among the Longhouse People during the 1400s. Peace, respect, and harmony are a way of life for the Longhouse People who reside in what is now New York State. Although brother and sister look alike, Ohkwa'ri acts before he thinks and Otsi:stia thinks before she acts. Otsi:stia is always watching out for Ohkwa'ri, even after Ohkwa'ri builds a lodge of his own. When Ohkwa'ri is given great honor by being asked to join the old men in a game of tekwaarathon, he becomes the target of increased contempt from a jealous older boy called Grabber. Ohkwa'ri is forced to ponder and then act upon the meaning of peace and respect when Grabber attempts to ambush him.

Hannah of Fairfield by Jean Van Leeuwen
Illustrated by Donna Diamond   Dial, 1999   GRADES 2–4

In this story of the Revolutionary War, nine-year-old Hannah must stay inside and knit while her brothers work outside and tend to the family farm. Then Hannah gets to feed a baby lamb and her family realizes her love of nature. When her brother Ben wants to join the colonial army, their father is at first set against his son going off to war. But as the British come closer to Fairfield, Ben gets his father's blessing. The family works hard to get ready for Ben's send off; Hannah works harder at her knitting and weaving and perhaps even grows wiser.

James Printer by Paul Samuel Jacobs
Scholastic, 1997   GRADES 5–8

Set during the English-Indian war that took place in 1674, this is the story of James Printer, an Indian raised as an Englishman who works as a printer's apprentice. Based on the real life of James Printer, this novel is told through the eyes of Bartholomew, the son of the printer to whom James is apprenticed. James is forced to choose sides when the colonists go to war with the local Indians.

Juliet: Midsummer at Greenchapel, England 1340 by Anna Kirwan
Illustrated by Lynne Marshall   Aladdin, 1997   GRADES 4–6

Juliet, a maid-in-waiting to Lady Marguerite D'Arsy, knows her place in the hierarchy of medieval society. When Gil, a falconer's son, is sent on a mission to fetch some medicine for an injured hawk, Juliet reluctantly volunteers to accompany him his trek. It's the day before Midsummer's Eve and everyone is planning on dancing and having fun around the bonfires that will be lit, but Juliet must go with Gil and perhaps miss all the fun. During her journey, Juliet realizes that she enjoys Gil's company too, and learns that there is more to life than the frivolities of society.

Keeping Room by Anna Myers
Walker, 1997   GRADES 4–6

Joey Kershaw is left in charge of the family home in Camden, South Carolina, when his father is taken prisoner during the Revolutionary War. General Cornwallis of the British army invades Camden and takes over the Kershaw home as his headquarters, where he begins hanging American prisoners. Joey plots to save his father from the gallows with a pistol he has hidden.

Midwife's Apprentice by Karen Cushman
Clarion, 1995   GRADES 6–10

Alyce, a young, homeless girl, becomes the apprentice to a midwife in this novel set in fourteenth-century England. It's a difficult life, especially when Alyce fails on her first outing as a midwife. Alyce runs away after her failure, but she picks herself up and gets back to work.

Winter Hare by Joan Elizabeth Goodman
Houghton Mifflin, 1996   GRADES 5–8

In twelfth-century England, Will Belet is sent to serve as a page in his uncle's household at Oxford. Although small and frail due to an illness when he was younger, Will has always dreamed of becoming a knight. But not until his traveling party is ambushed does he realize the horrors of war. Nicknamed "Rabbit" because of his size and weakness, Will must endure the hardships of being a page even though his older brother is already at Oxford. When Will realizes that he and his brother are in danger, his courage doesn't fail him. And in the most dangerous plot of all, Will must protect Empress Matilda by smuggling her out of Oxford Castle to safety.

25

Where Are Your Historical Fiction Books?

(Nineteenth Century)

Abraham's Battle: A Novel of Gettysburg by Sara Harrell Banks
Atheneum, 1999   GRADES 4–7

The battle of Gettysburg is brought to life in this brief novel that tells the story of former slave Abraham Small. Abraham has a chance encounter with a young Confederate soldier, Lamar, and they become friends. Their next meeting is during the battle of Gettysburg, where Abraham finds Lamar wounded. Abraham must choose whether to help his friend or let his enemy die.

Apprenticeship of Lucas Whitaker by Cynthia C. DeFelice
Farrar, Straus & Giroux, 1996   GRADES 5–8

Set in the mid-1800s, this is the story of Lucas Whitaker, who has lost all of his family to tuberculosis. He becomes apprentice to Dr. Uriah Beecher, a doctor, dentist, and undertaker. Lucas comes to believe the local custom that if you dig up the first family member to die of "consumption," remove and burn the heart, and breathe in the smoke then others in the family won't die from the disease.

Bandit's Moon by Sid Fleischman
Illustrated by Joseph A. Smith   Greenwillow, 1998   GRADES 4–7

See page 39 for a description of this book.

Bigger by Patricia Calvert
Atheneum, 1994   GRADES 5–8

At the end of the Civil War, Tyler Bohannon searches for his father who has joined a group of Confederate soldiers who are traveling to Mexico rather than live in defeat. On his trip from Missouri to the Rio Grande, Tyler picks up a stray dog that he names Bigger and dreams of a happy reunion with his father. But his father chooses to remain a soldier and Tyler must travel back home alone. The sequel is entitled *Sooner.*

Bright Freedom's Song: A Story of the Underground Railroad
by Gloria Houston   Harcourt, Brace, 1998   GRADES 4–6

Tension is mounting in the southern Appalachian Mountains during the early 1860s. Talk of secession permeates the air and slave hunters are everywhere. Bright Cameron is beginning to learn that there is a lot more to her family than she could ever imagine. When Bright finds Marcus, a former slave, hiding in the henhouse she begins to ask questions. When her ability to keep secrets is proven, Bright is made privy to her family's past and present; her father is a runaway indentured servant and he assists runaway slaves on their underground railroad journey. Bright must face her greatest challenge when her father takes ill and she and Marcus must transport three runaway slaves to safety.

Facing West: A Story of the Oregon Trail by Kathleen V. Kudlinski
Illustrated by James Watling   Viking, 1994   GRADES 3–5

Ben and his family join a wagon train that sets out for Oregon in 1845. Ben, who suffers from asthma, feels guilty that his family is making such a dangerous journey because the Oregon climate will be better for him. Ben learns to overcome his fears and to cope with his illness through his friendship with Pete, the leader of the wagon train. Part of the Once upon America series.

An Island Far from Home by John Donahue
Carolrhoda 1995   GRADES 4–7

Josh, whose father has been killed during the Civil War, is asked by his uncle to write to a young Confederate soldier at a prison camp. Although Josh is more intent on avenging his father's death, he agrees to write and eventually becomes friends with the prisoner. At the end of the war, Josh travels to the prison camp to meet his new friend.

Jayhawker by Patricia Beatty
Morrow, 1995   GRADES 5–8

Elijah Tulley and his family help to free slaves in Missouri before the Civil War. When the Bushwhackers kill his father during a raid, Lije is determined to become a Jayhawker, an abolitionist raider. After his farm is burned, Lije agrees to become a spy. Renamed Red, Lije infiltrates the Bushwhacker camp and pretends to be one of them. His dangerous assignment puts him in the company of Frank and Jesse James and Wild Bill Hickok.

Jip: His Story by Katherine Paterson
Lodestar, 1996   GRADES 5–9

Ever since he fell off the back of a wagon as a young child, Jip has lived on the town poor farm, hoping someone would come back to claim him. Now the townspeople have brought a lunatic to live on the farm, a deranged man, caged like an animal. Only Jip is brave enough and compassionate enough to treat the man, Putnam, as a human being. Jip comes to rely on Put as a friend when a stranger arrives in town asking questions about Jip and claiming to have been sent by Jip's father. As Jip puts together the pieces of his past, he realizes he is in great danger and help comes from unexpected sources.

Josefina Learns a Lesson: A School Story by Valerie Tripp
Illustrated by Jean-Paul Tibbles   Pleasant, 1997   GRADES 3–5

The youngest daughter of a Spanish rancher, nine-year-old Josefina Montoya lives with her four sisters in New Mexico in the 1800s. Josefina spends most of her life sewing and helping with chores. But when thunderous rain floods her village, the Montoyas lose a large number of sheep. With the help of her aunt, Tia Dolores, Josefina learns to weave cloth for blankets that will in turn be sold for new sheep. Without a mother, the four girls rely on Tia Dolores to teach them about running a household. When Tia Dolores announces that she will teach the girls to read, the girls are at first reluctant. Then Josefina realizes that she will be able to remember her mother by writing down words and phrases her mother used to say. Part of the American Girl series.

Journey to Nowhere by Mary Jane Auch
Henry Holt, 1997   GRADES 4–7

In 1815, Remembrance Nye and her family load up the wagon and head off to the wilderness of western New York. Along the way, Mem is separated from her family and is almost killed, first by a bear, then by a falling tree. The second book in this proposed trilogy is *Frozen Summer*.

Longwalker's Journey: A Novel of the Choctaw Trail of Tears by Beatrice Orcutt Harrell   Illustrated by Tony Meers   Dial, 1999   GRADES 3–5

Minko Ushi, a Choctaw Indian, is ten years old when his people are forced to relocate to the Oklahoma territory along the Trail of Tears.

Minko and his father decide to travel ahead with Minko's pony Black Spot. After walking hundreds of miles through winter storms, they build a new home and help the survivors recover from the arduous march. Based upon the true story of the author's ancestors.

Rachel's Journey by Marissa Moss
Silver Whistle, 1998　　　　　　　　　　　　　　　　GRADES 3–6

Rachel is ten years old when her family sets off in a covered wagon to travel from Illinois along the Oregon Trail to California in 1850. Rachel keeps a journal along the way chronicling her adventures with "illustrations" and "mementos."

Red Cap by G. Clifton Wisler
Lodestar 1991　　　　　　　　　　　　　　　　　　GRADES 4–7

Ransom Powell lies about his age when he joins the Union army during the Civil War. Ransom, now a drummer boy, is captured and ends up at the Confederate prison Andersonville. Based on a true story.

Soft Rain: A Story of the Cherokee Trail of Tears
by Cornelia Cornelissen　 Delacorte, 1998　　　　　　GRADES 4–6

Nine-year-old Soft Rain and her mother are forced to leave their beloved home and blind grandmother behind when white soldiers come and take them on a long journey west. Soft Rain is fearful that she will never see her father and brother again. When she loses her beloved cousin to illness, Soft Rain is in despair. But the women walk and endure the hardships on the trail, and Soft Rain realizes that going to school and learning the white man's words is beneficial. Reunited with her father and brother on the trail, the family heads west to the harsh land set aside for them by the government.

Three against the Tide by D. Anne Love
Holiday House, 1998　　　　　　　　　　　　　　　　GRADES 4–6

Susanna and her brothers are left on the family plantation in South Carolina when their father is called to assist the Confederate Army. When the Yankees invade their island, they must flee by riverboat to Charleston. When their house in Charleston goes up in flames, Susanna and her brothers leave Charleston to search for their father. In the face of danger, they finally reach their destination, find their father, and come to grips with their loss.

26

Where Are Your Historical Fiction Books?

(Twentieth Century)

Anna All Year Round by Mary Downing Hahn
Illustrated by Diane DeGroat Clarion, 1999 GRADES 6–8

A gentle story set during 1913 about eight-year-old Anna who lives in Baltimore. Anna struggles with arithmetic, secretly plans her birthday party against her mother's wishes, and takes a dare to roller-skate down the steepest hill in Baltimore.

Bat 6 by Virginia Euwer Wolff
Scholastic, 1998 GRADES 5–9

It's 1949 and the sixth grade girls from Barlow and Bear Creek Ridge, Oregon, are preparing for the annual Bat 6 softball game. Aki, a Japanese American who has spent six years in the internment camps, is one of the best players on the team. Shirley, nicknamed Shazam, is also playing, but her hatred for the Japanese because of her father's death at Pearl Harbor brings the game to a stunning halt.

Justice for Emily by Susan Beth Pfeffer
Delacorte, 1997 GRADES 4–6

In this story set in the early twentieth century, orphan Emily and her friends are taunted by the daughters of three prominent families. When the rich girls push Emily's friend to her death, Emily must face prejudice and ridicule for taking a stand and refusing to believe that the death was an accident. Sequel to *Nobody's Daughter*.

Lily's Crossing by Patricia Reilly Giff
Delacorte, 1997   GRADES 4–7

It's the summer of 1944 and Lily can't wait to go to Rockaway Beach, to her Gram's house on the Atlantic Ocean. Lily's best friend Margaret has moved away and her father has joined the war cause as an engineer for the Army. Lily spends her time alone, away from Gram, until she meets Albert, a Hungarian refugee. Albert has lost his parents to the war and was separated from his sister during their escape. When Albert tries to row by himself toward a ship, Lily must face the fact that her lies have endangered both her own life and Albert's.

Long Way from Chicago by Richard Peck
Dial, 1998   GRADES 5–8

Joey and his younger sister, Mary Alice, visit Grandma Dowdel every summer during the Depression. But she's not like any other grandma. She poaches catfish to feed the drifters, puts a dead mouse in a milk bottle for revenge, and carries a twelve-gauge shotgun.

Mayfield Crossing by Vaunda Micheaux Nelson
Putnam, 1993   GRADES 4–6

In the summer of 1960, the students of Mayfield Crossing are playing their last baseball game together. Meg and Billie and the rest of the Mayfield Crossing gang know everyone in their little community, even Old Hairy. There is no color barrier at Mayfield Crossing, everyone, black or white, plays together. In the fall, they are bused to a new school and Meg and Billie experience prejudice for the first time in their lives. When a bully accuses Meg of cheating and then tries to beat her up, Billie comes to her rescue. When the Parkview students refuse to let the Mayfield Crossing friends play ball, Billie comes up with a proposal they can't refuse.

Mieko and the Fifth Treasure by Eleanor Coerr
Calligraphy by H. Cecil Uyehara   Putnam, 1993   GRADES 3–5

Ten-year-old Mieko must leave her mother and father to stay with her grandparents after an atomic bomb hits Nagasaki in 1945. Before the bomb, Mieko was practicing the art of word pictures, and her art teacher said she possessed the fifth treasure, beauty in the heart. After the bomb, Mieko is filled with bitterness as her hand is badly cut and scarred. She can no longer practice the word pictures and the students in her new school make fun of her and her hand. When Mieko sees Yoshi, a girl from school, she begins to look forward to their meetings. Soon Mieko is back at school and learning to write with a pencil. When her teacher announces a word picture contest, Mieko is not sure she should enter because she has lost the fifth treasure. With help from Yoshi and her grandparents, Mieko's bitterness finally dissolves.

My Louisiana Sky by Kimberly Willis Holt
Holt, 1998   GRADES 4–7

Tiger Ann Parker is a straight A student who lives in Louisiana in the 1950s with her mentally challenged parents and grandmother. When her grandmother dies of a heart attack, Tiger Ann is invited to go live with her Aunt Doreen in Baton Rouge. She sees a chance to start over and get away from the humiliation of having "slow" parents. But Tiger Ann learns to appreciate her parents in this beautifully written coming-of-age novel.

Night Crossing by Karen Ackerman
Illustrated by Elizabeth Sayles   Knopf, 1995   GRADES 2–5

Clara and her family must leave their home in Innsbruck, Austria, when the Nazis begin sending Jews to the concentration camps. They sell most of their belongings except for the Sabbath candlesticks and two dolls that Clara's grandmother brought with her from Russia. The family escapes into the night to travel over the mountains to Switzerland.

Out of the Dust by Karen Hesse
Scholastic, 1997   GRADES 5–7

Told in the form of poetic journal entries, this is the story of Billie Jo, a fourteen-year-old who lives in Oklahoma during the Great Depression. Her mother dies in a fire, which also scars Billie Jo's hands, leaving her unable to play the piano any more. As her father becomes more remote, Billie Jo decides to jump a train and head west.

Spying on Miss Muller by Eve Bunting
Illustrated by Ellen Thompson   Clarion, 1995   GRADES 5–8

Jesse is a thirteen-year-old student at boarding school in Ireland during World War II. Amidst air raids and bomb shelters, the school and students survive. Jesse and her friends suspect their teacher Miss Muller of being a German spy because her father is a Nazi. When Jesse sees Miss Muller climb up to the tower at night and bombs are dropped on Belfast the next day, she is suspicious and the girls decide to follow their teacher. What they find is far from what they expected.

Stones in Water by Donna Jo Napoli
Dutton, 1997   GRADES 6–8

See page 49 for a description of this book.

The Watsons Go to Birmingham—1963
by Christopher Paul Curtis   Delacorte, 1995   GRADES 4–8

Kenny Watson has a tough older brother named Byron who is always in trouble in their hometown of Flint, Michigan. Kenny's parents decide that Grandma Sands will straighten Byron out, so they head off for Birmingham, Alabama, in 1963. Hilariously funny at the beginning, this novel becomes more serious as Kenny and his African-American family learn firsthand about racism and the Civil Rights movement.

The Well: David's Story by Mildred D. Taylor
Dial, 1995   GRADES 5–7

David Logan (the father in *Roll of Thunder, Hear My Cry*) is a young boy in this story set during a drought. The Logans are willing to share the water from their well with their neighbors, black and white, but some of the white neighbors are unwilling to depend on the charity of black people. David and his brother Hammer are confronted by mean Charlie Simms in a violent climax.

27

Where Are Your Animal Books?

(Picture Books)

The Bat in the Boot by Annie Cannon
Orchard, 1996   GRADE K

> When a young girl and her brother find a bat in their father's boot, they put it in a shoebox and feed it milk with an eyedropper. When darkness arrives, the siblings are surprised to find the mother bat streaking through the open window. They ease off the lid of the shoebox and the bat disappears into the night sky with her baby.

The Bear That Heard Crying by Natalie Kinsey-Warnock and
Helen Kinsey   Illustrated by Ted Rand   Cobblehill, 1993   GRADES K–3

> Three-year-old Sarah Whitcher follows her parents into the woods but gets distracted by wild strawberries and picking flowers. Soon she is lost. Her parents, friends, and neighbors search for her for four days. They find many bear tracks, but they do not find Sarah. When she is found, Sarah tells everyone about the "big black dog" that kept her warm at night. Based on a true story.

Chato's Kitchen by Gary Soto
Illustrated by Susan Guevara   Putnam, 1995   GRADES K–3

> See page 1 for a description of this book.

Gemma and the Baby Chick by Antonia Barber
Illustrated by Karin Littlewood   Scholastic, 1992   GRADES K–3

> Gemma comes home from school one day to find that one of their hens is sitting on her eggs and will not move. Gemma's mother says that the hen has gone "broody" and fixes up a special nesting box for the hen. For three weeks, Gemma waits for the eggs to hatch. And one morning, she

finds the hen surrounded by gray and yellow fuzzballs—seven new chicks! But what about the eggs that are left in the nest? Can Gemma and her mother save the chicks that did not hatch?

Gracias the Thanksgiving Turkey by Joy Cowley
Illustrated by Joe Cepeda   Scholastic, 1996   GRADES K–3

When Miguel goes to the train station to pick up a present from his dad, he is quite surprised to find a turkey in a crate! The note from his dad says to fatten up the turkey for Thanksgiving. Miguel's grandparents and aunt are not pleased about having a turkey around their small apartment. But Miguel takes good care of the turkey and soon everyone in the neighborhood helps out too. Miguel starts worrying though when everyone talks about how the turkey is getting too big to fit into the oven. Miguel does not want to eat his pet for Thanksgiving. What will he do?

Only a Pigeon by Jane and Christopher Kurtz
Illustrated by E. B. Lewis   Simon & Schuster, 1997   GRADES K–3

Ondu-ahlem lives in Addis Ababa, Ethiopia, where he spends his days attending school and trying to earn a little pocket money. He devotes all his free time, however, to caring for the homing pigeons he is raising. Every day he must feed them and make sure their eggs are safe and warm. At night, he must protect the birds from the mongoose that frequently threatens them. Ondu-ahlem is modeled after a real boy the Kurtzes knew when they were living in Ethiopia.

Tale of a Tadpole by Barbara Ann Porte
Illustrated by Annie Cannon   Orchard, 1997   GRADES K–3

Francine has a tadpole named Fred. The people at the nature center give her advice on what to feed him and how to care for him. Francine waits every day for Fred to get feet and to turn into a frog. Her sister teases her about kissing Fred to turn him into a prince instead. When Grandma and Grandpa come for a visit, Francine finds out something very interesting about Fred.

28

Where Are Your Animal Books?

(Chapter Books)

Booford Summer by Susan Mathias Smith
Illustrated by Andrew Glass   Clarion, 1994   GRADES 3–6

Hayley loves animals and has five cats. When Mr. Wood moves in across
the road, she can't help wanting to make friends with his dog, Booford.
Mr. Wood keeps Booford tied up to a doghouse all the time and does not
take him for walks. Hayley never sees Mr. Wood pet Booford, either, or
speak kindly to him. How can Hayley help Booford when her parents
have told her to stay away from Mr. Wood's place?

Bunnicula Strikes Again! by James Howe
Illustrated by Alan Daniel   Atheneum, 1999   GRADES 4–6

Once again Bunnicula is sucking up all the vegetable juice. This time
Chester the cat is determined to stop him for good. When Bunnicula is
rushed off to the vet, Chester, Harold, and Howie follow behind. Chester
and Bunnicula end up trapped in an old movie theater that is about to be
demolished.

The Cuckoo Child by Dick King-Smith
Illustrated by Leslie W. Bowman   Hyperion, 1993   GRADES 5–7

Jack Daw loves birds. And on the farm where he lives with his family, he
has lots of birds: ducks, chickens, and geese. But when his class visits the
Wildlife Park, he encounters a bird like nothing he has ever seen before—
an ostrich! Jack is so amazed by this tremendous bird that he steals an
ostrich egg that is about to be discarded and tricks his pet geese into
hatching it. Jack names the baby ostrich Oliver and persuades his parents
to let him raise this peculiar-looking bird.

Flatfoot Fox and the Case of the Nosy Otter by Eth Clifford
Illustrated by Brian Lies   Houghton Mifflin, 1992   GRADES 2–4

Flatfoot Fox, the smartest detective in the whole world, is on another case. According to his mother, Mrs. Chatterbox Otter, Nosy Otter has been kidnapped. Flatfoot Fox and his assistant, Secretary Bird, search for clues that they hope will lead to Nosy Otter. But will Chatterbox Otter stop talking? Crabby Crow agrees to be an air scout if Mrs. Chatterbox can promise to stop talking for twenty-four hours. While Crabby Crow is in the air, Flatfoot Fox and Secretary Bird follow the footprints that lead them to a worried woodchuck, a lame-brain swan, and finally a motherly mouse with Nosy Otter in her house.

Gooseberry Park by Cynthia Rylant
Illustrated by Arthur Howard   Harcourt, Brace, 1995   GRADES 3–5

Kona, a labrador retreiver, lives with Professor Albert and Gwendolyn, a hermit crab. Kona has another friend too; Stumpy is a red squirrel who lives in Gooseberry Park. Stumpy is busy because she just had three babies. One night an ice storm comes and breaks Stumpy's tree in half. Kona is worried about Stumpy and her babies and goes out to the park to see if they are okay. Kona finds the babies, but not Stumpy. Where can Stumpy be? And how can Kona take care of the babies?

Lolo and Red-Legs by Kirk Reeve
Rising Moon, 1998   GRADES 4–6

Lolo is thrilled to find a tarantula near the fort he and his friends are building in their East Los Angeles neighborhood. His mother, however, is not at all thrilled and she won't let Lolo bring the tarantula into the house. But with the help of his grandfather and a knowledgeable pet-store owner, Lolo figures out a way to keep "Red-Legs" safe in his fort— that is, until some older boys destroy the fort and Red-Legs disappears.

The Mouse of Amherst by Elizabeth Spires   Illustrated by
Claire A. Nivola   Farrar, Straus, & Giroux, 1999   GRADES 4–6

When Emmaline, a white mouse, moves into a house in Amherst, she begins a correspondence with Emily Dickinson. As she prefers quiet quarters, Emmaline moves into the upstairs bedroom of Emily Dickinson herself. A note left by the previous tenant intrigues Emmaline and when she reads a scrap of Emily's poetry, Emmaline is compelled to put her own words to paper. With snippets of Emily Dickinson's poetry, this sweet story tells how Emily and Emmaline interact with one another. Emily even saves Emmaline from a weasel sent to snuff the mouse out. When Emmaline decides to leave the house on Main Street, she takes her memories with her in a little book.

Mr. Putter and Tabby Walk the Dog by Cynthia Rylant
Illustrated by Arthur Howard   Harcourt, Brace, 1994   GRADES K–2

Mr. Putter is a little deaf with thinning hair and so is his cat Tabby. They live next door to Mrs. Teaberry and her dog Zeke. One day, Mrs. Teaberry slips and hurts her foot. Who will walk her lollypup Zeke if she can't walk for a week? Mr. Putter and Tabby volunteer. But Zeke is a nightmare until he and Mr. Putter make a deal.

Poppy by Avi
Illustrated by Brian Floca   Orchard, 1995   GRADES 4–6

See page 41 for a description of this book.

Spotting the Leopard by Anna Myers   Walker, 1996   GRADES 4–6

In this story set in the 1930s, H. J. is worried about his sister's dream of becoming a veterinarian. Sure, Jessie has a way with animals. Didn't she help their dog, Ring, when he got bitten by the copperhead? But H. J. has never heard of a woman veterinarian before and their family does not have enough money for Jessie's schooling anyway. But when a leopard goes missing from the local zoo, H. J. sees a chance not only to help the endangered leopard, but also to help out his sister Jessie.

There's an Owl in the Shower by Jean Craighead George
Illustrated by Christine Herman Merrill
HarperCollins, 1995   GRADES 3–5

Borden's dad has lost his job and it's all because of the spotted owl. Borden's dad is a logger and he is out of work because the northern spotted owl is a threatened species. One day, Borden discovers an owlet that fell out of its nest and was left to die. Thinking it's a barred owl, he takes it home to feed it until it can fly back to its natural habitat. To everyone's amazement, Borden's dad becomes attached to the owl and the owl to his dad. Soon, the owl becomes a regular member of the family. It watches television and takes showers and to everyone's surprise, grows up be a strong spotted owl. Hatred and revenge are erased through caring for a small helpless animal.

Upchuck and Rotten Willy by Bill Wallace
Illustrated by David Slonin   Pocket Books, 1998   GRADES 3–5

Chuck, the cat, enjoys his life with his feline friend Tom. They tease the neighboring poodles, beg for food at Luigi's Restaurant, and talk about Louie, their friend who was struck by a car. Life goes on as usual until they meet a monster named Rotten Willy. Only Rotten Willy is not a monster, he's a rottweiler. Eventually Chuck realizes that no matter how different, cats and dogs can get along.

Wainscott Weasel by Tor Seidler
Illustrated by Fred Marcellino   HarperCollins, 1993   GRADES 4–6

Wendy Blackish moves to Wainscott to live with her aunt and uncle. At the first dance of the season, Wendy hopes to meet Bagley Jr., the son of the famous Bagley Brown. She does meet the young Bagley, the mysterious weasel who wears an eyepatch. But first she meets Zeke, a brash young male, not favored by her uncle. While Wendy is torn between her affections for Bagley and Zeke, Bagley falls in love with the beautiful Bridget. Bridget, however, is a fish so there is little hope of Bagley finding happiness. Or is there?

The Warm Place by Nancy Farmer
Orchard, 1995   GRADES 4–7

Ruva, a young giraffe, is taken from her mother and her home in Africa. She is then sent by ship to a zoo in San Francisco. She misses her mother and longs to return to Africa. With help from Troll, a rat, and Nelson, a chameleon, Ruva hopes to find her way back home.

The Willows in Winter by William Horwood
St. Martin's, 1994   GRADES 4–7

The characters from Kenneth Graham's classic book, *The Wind in the Willows*, live on in this new book written as a sequel. Rat, Mole, Badger, and Toad are good friends through thick and thin. When Mole disappears in a blizzard, all the residents of the woods get involved in searching for him, even the weasels. Bored with the dreary task of searching on the ground and underground, Toad takes to the air in his new airplane and lands in a heap of trouble. Will they ever find Mole again? And how will Toad get out of trouble this time?

29

Where Are Your Cat Stories?

(Picture Books)

Bimmi Finds a Cat by Elisabeth Jane Stewart
Illustrated by James Ransome   Clarion, 1996   GRADES K–2

> After the loss of his own cat, eight-year-old Bimmi is pleased to come across a stray cat, which he names Kitty-Louise. But after he takes her home, he realizes there may be someone out there who misses this new cat as much as Bimmi misses his old one. Bimmi's search for the cat's owner leads to a satisfying reward.

Black Cat by Christopher Myers
Scholastic, 1999   GRADES K–4

> From a cat's point of view, a big city consists of a maze of fences and walls, asphalt and garbage cans. Stunning collage illustrations and a brief rhyming text trace the path of a small black cat, wending his way through city streets throughout a day and night.

Cat up a Tree by John and Ann Hassett
Houghton Mifflin, 1998   GRADES K–3

> Nana Quimby sees a cat up a tree and she calls the fire department. But the fire department tells her to call back if she sees the cat playing with matches. When she returns to the window, she finds five cats up a tree, so she calls the police. The police inform her that they do not catch cats up trees, that she should call them if the cats rob a bank. Each time Nana Quimby goes to the window there are more cats in this clever feline counting story.

Comet's Nine Lives by Jan Brett
Putnam, 1996   GRADES K–3

Comet the cat was born on Nantucket Island. One day, he decides to taste foxgloves and falls into a deep sleep. When he wakes up, he realizes that one of his nine lives is gone. When Comet decides to settle down on a tower of books, he is content. That is, until the tower of books topples. There goes life number two. Comet loses six more lives—then realizes finally that he is home and where he wants to live the rest of his life.

Ginger by Charlotte Voake
Candlewick, 1997   GRADES K–3

Ginger the cat has a very fine life until a kitten moves in. The little girl thinks that the kitten will be a good new friend for Ginger. But the kitten springs out from behind doors and eats Ginger's food. So Ginger decides to run away. After the little girl finds Ginger, she gives Ginger and the new kitten each a bowl for food and a place to sleep. Soon Ginger and the kitten are friends.

The Good Luck Cat by Joy Harjo
Illustrated by Paul Lee   Harcourt, Brace, 2000   GRADES K–3

Aunt Shelly claims that Woogie is a good-luck cat because he is always able to get himself out of any fix he gets himself into. His good luck will also rub off on everyone who pets him. But when Woogie doesn't come home one night, everyone wonders if his luck has finally run out.

Henry the Sailor Cat by Mary Calhoun
Illustrated by Erick Ingraham   Morrow, 1994   GRADES K–3

When Henry the cat stows away on a sailboat with the boy and the man, he can't wait to see dolphins and whales. But storm clouds are rolling in fast and when the man falls into the water, only Henry sees him. Henry claws the line on the tiller to make the boat stop. Then he points with his body to indicate where the man is. The man is rescued and the boy tells his dad all about Henry's heroic cat deeds.

Leo the Magnificat by Ann M. Martin
Illustrated by Emily McCully   Scholastic, 1996   GRADES K–3

Leo the cat just showed up one day at the church. Leo enjoys his life at the church. He attends meetings, choir practices, covered-dish dinners, and even church services. But one day Leo gives everyone a scare when he doesn't show up for his meals. Luckily, a taxi driver brings him home and Leo never misses another meal.

The Loyal Cat by Lensey Namioka   Illustrated by
Aki Sogabe   Browndeer/Harcourt, Brace, 1995   GRADES K–3

Holy man Tetsuzan lives a simple life in a Japanese temple, caring little for fame or material wealth. When a magical cat called Huku shows up one day, he decides to upgrade Tetsuzan's life a bit. Based on a traditional Japanese tale about greed and humility, this beautifully illustrated picture book combines elegance with humor.

Pandora by William Mayne
Illustrated by Dietlind Blech   Knopf, 1995   GRADES K–3

Pandora is a happy black cat until something new comes into the house. Soon, Pandora is put outside looking in at the new baby. One day, feeling unloved, Pandora leaves her home. She grows wild in the wilderness, living in a cave and learning to hunt for her meals. Then one night, Pandora has kittens of her own. Now Pandora understands. When she returns to her home, she and her kittens are welcomed with warm milk.

Rotten Ralph's Rotten Romance by Jack Gantos
Illustrated by Nicole Rubel   Houghton Mifflin, 1997   GRADES K–3

Rotten Ralph has to go to a Valentine's Day party with Sarah. So, Rotten Ralph decides to be his rottenest. Ralph eats the cherries from Sarah's chocolate covered cherries and puts in ants. At the party, Rotten Ralph breaks all the candy hearts in half. When Petunia tells Ralph to kiss her, he throws his love arrows across the room and soon is smothered in kisses. But dog food smeared on Ralph's face ends anyone's notion of kissing him again. Rotten Ralph is indeed rotten.

Six-Dinner Sid by Inga Moore
Simon & Schuster, 1991   GRADES K–3

Sid was a sly cat. He lived at six different houses on Aristotle Street and got fed six different times. Of course, Sid had six names. He was swanky as Scaramouche, naughty as Mischief, and silly as Sally. He was scratched in six different places and had six different beds. Sid had it made. Until one day Sid developed a nasty cough and Sid went to the veterinarian six different times. The doctor discovered what Sid had been up to and called the neighbors. They decided to give Sid only one meal a day. So, Sid moved on—to six new houses.

Tonio's Cat by Mary Calhoun
Illustrated by Edward Martinez   Morrow, 1996   GRADES K–3

Tonio has just moved from Mexico to California, and, as a newcomer, he feels lonely at school and in his new neighborhood. His loneliness causes him to befriend a stray cat by feeding him scraps of food, which in turn makes it a bit easier for him to talk to other kids who stop to admire his feline friend. Gradually Tonio begins to feel a bit more at home in his new life.

30

Where Are
Your Cat Stories?

(Chapter Books)

Callie and Zora by Barbara Burris
Illustrated by Wendy Halstead   Pennyroyal, 1998   GRADES 3–5

> In this sweet Christmas story, Zora is a sad young girl with little joy in her
> life until she meets Callie, an abandoned calico kitten. As Zora's love for
> Callie grows, she learns how much this little cat can teach her about sur-
> viving and loving others.

Casebook of a Private (Cat's) Eye by Mary Stolz
Illustrated by Pamela R. Levy   Front Street, 1999   GRADES 3–6

> Eileen O'Kelly is a cat detective who lives in Boston in 1912. In this
> humorous collection of cases, young readers will enjoy getting to know
> the feline detective as she finds a lox thief and a catnip crook and solves
> a murder.

Cat's Meow by Gary Soto
Illustrated by Joe Cepeda   Scholastic, 1995   GRADES 3–5

> In this unusual story, third-grader Graciela thinks her cat, Pip, is speak-
> ing Spanish. When she tries to tell her parents and her friend Juanita, Pip
> keeps quiet. When Pip tells Graciela that Mr. Medina has taught her
> Spanish, Graciela has to find out more about this mysterious man.

Courtyard Cat by C. S. Adler
Illustrated by Robina McIntyre   Clarion, 1995   GRADES 4–6

> Eleven-year-old Lindsay has moved from the country to New York City
> so her younger brother can be close to the hospital. Lindsay feels respon-
> sible for her brother's accident that requires so much treatment. With the

help of a homeless cat that lives in the courtyard outside her apartment, Lindsay finds new friends.

Ghost Eye by Marion Dane Bauer
Illustrated by Trina Schart Hyman   Scholastic, 1992   GRADES 4–6

Purrloom Popcorn is a special cat. He is a Cornish rex, has won numerous blue ribbons in cat shows, and has one gold and one blue eye. When Popcorn is taken from his cattery and returned to his original home, he is unhappy. He now has to live with a girl named Melinda who does not appreciate his specialness. The only thing Popcorn wants to do is run away. Then he finds that his blue eye is a ghost eye and he can see ghosts. As Popcorn meets the former cats and then aunt Lydia, the original owner of both Popcorn and the house, he feels some solace and eventually realizes that he is where he needed to be all along.

The Healing of Texas Jake by Phyllis Reynolds Naylor
Illustrated by Alan Daniel   Atheneum, 1997   GRADES 3–6

Marco and Polo are back in this sequel to *The Grand Escape*. This time they have to help the leader of the Club of Mysteries, Texas Jake, recover from the wounds he received in a fight with a dog. To prove their loyalty to Texas Jake, they have to sneak into the town dump to retrieve an herb that heals wounds. However, a rival gang led by the ruthless cat Steak Knife controls the dump.

Jane on Her Own: A Catwings Tale by Ursula K. Le Guin
Illustrated by S. D. Schindler   Orchard, 1999   GRADES 2–4

See page 32 for a description of this book.

Minnie by Annie M. G. Schmidt. Translated by Lance Salway
Illustrated by Kay Sather   Milkweed, 1994   GRADES 3–6

Miss Minnie was a cat, but now she's a human with some very cat-like tendencies. She still climbs trees to get away from dogs. She likes to root around in the garbage for fish bones and she can still talk to cats. When Mr. Tibbs, a newspaperman who likes to write about cats, rescues Miss Minnie from the tree, they become friends. Miss Minnie helps Mr. Tibbs by bringing him all the cat gossip from the neighborhood.

Three Stories You Can Read to Your Cat by Sara Swan Miller
Illustrated by True Kelley   Houghton Mifflin, 1997   GRADES 1–3

Very young readers will enjoy their first chapter book about being a cat in this companion book to *Three Stories You Can Read to Your Dog* (*see* p. 4). The three humorous episodes accompanied by True Kelley's amusing illustrations are fun to share aloud with young elementary students.

Yang the Third and Her Impossible Family by Lensey Namioka
Illustrated by Kees de Kiefte   Little, Brown, 1995   GRADES 3–6

The second in the popular series about the Yang family, which has moved from China to Seattle, features the third child, Yingmei, who works hard to fit in among her new American friends. But Yingmei's biggest challenge is in getting her parents to allow her to have a pet cat. In fact, she's already accepted a kitten from her friend, Holly, and she and her younger brother, Yingtao, struggle to keep the kitten's presence in their household a secret from the rest of the family, hoping their parents will eventually give in.

31

Where Are
Your Dog Stories?
(Picture Books)

Amos Camps Out by Susan Seligman and Howie Schneider
Little, Brown, 1992   GRADES K–3

Amos is an old dog that loves his couch. Amos's couch moves and takes
him anywhere he wants to go. When the Bobsons decide to take Amos on
a camping trip, Amos is excited. Until, that is, he finds out he has to sleep
in a tent and there are no sidewalks or streets to follow to guide him
home. One night, Amos discovers that something is stealing his beloved
hot dogs. What could it be?

Bookshop Dog by Cynthia Rylant
Blue Sky, 1996   GRADES K–3

Once there was a woman who loved her dog so much that she took her
everywhere—even to work. That woman owned a bookshop and changed
the name of her shop to Martha Jane's Bookshop, in honor of her dog.
Martha Jane's popularity makes business good for the bookshop, but also
makes trouble when the woman needs a sitter for Martha Jane. Who will
get to keep the beloved Martha Jane while the woman goes into the hospital to have her tonsils out? Will the postman keep Martha Jane? Or the
policeman, or the children, or the band director?

Digby by Barbara Shook Hazen
Illustrated by Barbara Phillips-Duke   HarperCollins, 1997   GRADES K–2

An "I Can Read" book that features a realistic conversation between a little brother and big sister who love their dog, Digby, even though she can
no longer run, jump, and play ball as she could when she was younger.

Dog Breath! The Horrible Trouble with Hally Tosis
by Dav Pilkey   Scholastic, 1994   GRADES K–3

See page 2 for a description of this book.

Dog Magic by Carla Golembe
Houghton Mifflin, 1997   GRADES K–2

Molly's fear of dogs seems to vanish magically when she puts on her new turquoise shoes. Soon she befriends every dog in her neighborhood. But what will happen when she outgrows her magic shoes?

The Dog Who Had Kittens by Polly Robertus
Illustrated by Janet Stevens   Holiday House, 1991   GRADES K–3

Baxter is a basset hound whose life is disrupted by kittens. When Eloise has kittens, Baxter has to stay in the garage. When Baxter is finally let into the house, he hears the cries of the kittens. Eloise is nowhere in sight. So Baxter does the only thing he can think of, he climbs in the box with the kittens. When Eloise comes back, she is furious.

A Home for Spooky by Gloria Rand
Illustrated by Ted Rand   Henry Holt, 1998   GRADES 2–4

Annie sees a stray dog while riding her bike home from school. Although the dog backs away from her when she approaches it, she names it Spooky. Fearing that her parents won't let her have another pet, Annie tells no one about Spooky. Every day after school and on weekends, Annie visits Spooky and leaves food for him. One day, Annie finds Spooky lying by the road and she must find help. Based on a true story.

Jojofu by Michael P. Waite
Illustrated by Yoriko Ito   Lothrop, Lee & Shepard, 1996   GRADES 2–4

This picture book based on a Japanese folktale tells the story of the faithful hunting dog Jojofu, who heroically protects her master, Takumi, during a hunting trip by keeping him from stepping off the side of a cliff in a deep fog and by fighting a large snake that attacks him.

Martha Speaks by Susan Meddaugh
Houghton Mifflin, 1992   GRADES K–3

Martha is a dog who, after eating alphabet soup, learns to speak. Of course, Martha's family has to ask her all sorts of questions and she, in

return, asks them questions of her own. Unfortunately, once Martha
starts talking, she can't stop. When her family can no longer take the constant chatter, they tell Martha to stop talking. This hurts Martha's feelings. She refuses to talk, she refuses to eat, and she refuses to do anything
until a burglar unknowingly gives her a bowl of alphabet soup!

Maxi the Hero by Debra and Sal Barracca
Illustrated by Mark Buehner   Dial, 1991   GRADES K–3

Maxi, from *The Adventures of Taxi Dog,* is back driving around the city
with Jim in a big taxi. In this story in rhyme, they meet sailors, a chef with
a tray of spaghetti, and triplets named Ed, Ned, and Fred. When Maxi and
Jim hear someone yell, "stop thief," Maxi takes off in search of the man
who stole a purse. The man slips on a peel with Maxi at his heel. He gives
Maxi a fight but Maxi holds on tight and the next day Maxi's picture is in
the paper.

McDuff and the Baby by Rosemary Wells
Hyperion, 1997   GRADES K–3

McDuff lives with Lucy and Fred. Fred reads the comics to McDuff in the
mornings. In the afternoons, Lucy takes McDuff for walks in the woods.
Soon though, Lucy and Fred do not have time to do these things with
McDuff any more. They must take care of the baby. Poor McDuff! The
baby pulls his fur. McDuff becomes so sad that he stops eating. But Lucy
and Fred know just what to do to make him feel better again.

My Buddy by Audrey Osofsky
Henry Holt, 1992   GRADES K–3

For a boy with muscular dystrophy, a golden retriever is much more than
a pet. Buddy is a service dog. He helps the boy by carrying his books to
school, turning on the light for him, and even going shopping with him.
This book describes Buddy's training and his life with the boy who needs
his help and the bond that makes them buddies.

The Night I Followed the Dog by Nina Laden
Chronicle, 1994   GRADES 1–3

A boy thinks he has a boring, ordinary dog until he follows his dog into
the night. Soon, the boy discovers that his dog has a doghouse with a living room, bathroom, and huge closet. Wearing a tuxedo, the dog jumps

into a limousine and heads to an empty building where dogs can be dogs. No leashes, no rules, no sitting, no begging, no masters.

Officer Buckle and Gloria by Peggy Rathmann
Putnam, 1995   GRADES K–3

See page 3 for a description of this book.

The Outside Dog by Charlotte Pomerantz
Illustrated by Jennifer Plecas   HarperCollins, 1993   GRADES K–2

Marisol lives with her grandfather in Puerto Rico and she desperately wants a dog. But Grandfather says, "No!" Even so, she begins to make friends with one of the stray dogs that roam over the hillside near their home. Before long, Marisol is petting this dog and feeding it scraps. Soon, her *abuelito* agrees to buy dog food and a collar for the dog, now named Pancho. Will Marisol really get to keep Pancho? She finds out when Pancho is lost, and Grandfather helps her look for him.

Three Names by Patricia MacLachlan
Illustrated by Alexander Pertzoff   HarperCollins, 1991   GRADES K–3

A boy's great-grandfather reminisces about a dog with Three Names. The dog was called Ted, Boots, and Pal as well as Three Names, which makes four. The dog was a faithful companion to Great-grandfather, accompanying him and his siblings to school. At the end of the school year, after the snow and tornadoes and storms, Great-grandfather and Three Names are both sad. They'll have to wait a whole summer before school starts again.

Walter's Tail by Lisa Campbell Ernst
Bradbury, 1992   GRADES K–3

Mrs. Tully lives alone with Walter, her dog. When Walter was a puppy, everyone adored his cute little waggling, constantly moving, tail. The trouble starts when Walter and his tail grow. When Walter accidentally knocks over displays at the grocery store, when flowers lose their petals at the florist, and when cakes vanish at the baker's, Walter and his tail are deemed a nuisance. Not until Walter's tail saves Mrs. Tully do the townspeople realize the true value of Walter's tail.

32

Where Are Your Dog Stories?

(Chapter Books)

Buster: The Very Shy Dog by Lisze Bechtold
Houghton Mifflin, 1999   GRADES 1–2

> Three short chapters tell the story of Buster, a shy dog. He lives with his owner Roger, another dog named Phoebe, three cats, and a hamster. Phoebe bosses him around and so do the cats. Buster wonders what he is good at until he realizes that every dog is special in his or her own way.

Chuck and Danielle by Peter Dickinson
Illustrated by Kees de Kiefte   Delacorte, 1996   GRADES 4–6

> Danielle's whippet Chuck is afraid of everything: paper bags, loud noises, motorcycles, cats, and even stuffed animals. Unfortunately, Chuck's favorite place to hide when she is scared is between the legs of whoever is near. Danielle's mother threatens to get rid of Chuck because of her tendency to knock people and things over in her wild attempts to get away from whatever is scaring her. But Danielle is sure that one day, Chuck will save the universe. Chuck and Danielle have many adventures and maybe Chuck does save the universe after all. Well, kind of.

Dog Crazy by Eve B. Feldman
Illustrated by Eric Jon Nones   Tambourine, 1992   GRADES 3–4

> Sara Fine desperately wants a dog. She reads dog books, draws dog pictures, and dreams of the day when she has one of her very own. She just knows she's getting a dog for her birthday and when she receives a wooden dog puppet instead, she is devastated. Then Sara hatches a plan. If she treats her puppet like a real dog, her parents may think she's going crazy and they'll just have to get her a real one.

Dog Friday by Hilary McKay
Margaret K. McElderry, 1994 GRADES 4–6

Ten-year-old Robin Brogan lives a quiet life with his mother on the coast of England. After an unfortunate run-in with a dog, Robin is terrified of them. When new neighbors move in next door, Robin's life changes forever. The neighbors are not like anyone Robin has ever met. They have funny names: Ant for Antoinette and Perry for Peregrine, Beany and Sun Dance and a dog named Old Blanket. When Robin finds an abandoned dog starving on the beach, he overcomes his fear with the help of his new friends.

Dog People: Native American Dog Stories by Joseph Bruchac
Illustrated by Murv Jacob   Fulcrum Kids, 1995 GRADES 4–6

This book contains stories about the Abnaki people and their companion dogs living about ten thousand years ago in the area that is now northern New England. In these stories, Joseph Bruchac tells the stories in the voice of a storyteller in that long-ago age when dogs and children shared a close relationship. According to Abnaki legend, Dog People are intelligent beings that have chosen to live with humans. Just as people are given names that reflect their personality or looks, so are dogs. Includes a glossary of names and words.

Dogs of Myth: Tales from Around the World by Gerald and
Loretta Hausman   Illustrated by Barry Moser
Simon & Schuster, 1999 GRADES 4–7

Thirteen traditional tales from diverse cultural sources show magical and mythic canine characters, including dogs as guardians, tricksters, and ghosts. Beautifully illustrated with watercolor paintings by Barry Moser.

Faith and the Electric Dogs by Patrick Jennings
Scholastic, 1996 GRADES 3–5

See page 5 for a description of this book.

The Great Genghis Khan Look-Alike Contest by Marjorie Sharmat
Illustrated by Mitchell Rigie   Random, 1993 GRADES 2–3

When a mean-looking dog follows Fred home, he realizes that Duz is not mean at all. In fact, Duz just may be too nice to enter the Genghis Khan

Look-Alike contest. But Fred is getting more and more in debt now that he owes his parents money for Duz's upkeep. So, Fred decides to find a way for Duz to get a job so he can pay his own expenses. After submitting a photo of Duz, Fred waits to see if Duz makes it as a finalist. He does, and the family flies off to Hollywood for an audition. Will Duz be able to imitate that famous Genghis Khan growl? A First Stepping Stone book.

Latchkey Dog by Mary Jane Auch
Illustrated by Bowman Smith   Little, Brown, 1994   GRADES 3–4

Sam has a problem. His dog Amber barks all day long while he and his little sister Maxie are at school. The next-door neighbor is complaining and Sam's mother is saying that Amber has to be given away. How can Sam give away Amber when she has been part of the family ever since Sam was born? With help from his friend Jamie, Sam comes up with some interesting but unworkable schemes. All are forlorn until the family comes up with a clever way of dealing with their latchkey dog.

Lucky in Left Field by Betsy Duffey
Illustrated by Leslie Morrill   Simon & Schuster, 1992   GRADES 2–4

Lucky *is* a lucky dog! School is out and he plays baseball every day with his owner George. Lucky plays left field with the Expos, a team that has yet to win a game. Lucky is in heaven—until Chet, a college student who is home for the summer and has agreed to coach the Expos, arrives, that is. Unfortunately, Chet refuses to have a dog on the team. When Lucky is lost, George realizes that Chet isn't always right and that dogs do belong in left field.

Not My Dog by Colby Rodowsky   Illustrated by Thomas F.
Yezerski   Farrar, Straus, & Giroux, 1999   GRADES 3–5

Eight-year-old Ellie Martin has been wanting a puppy for as long as she can remember. Her parents have promised that she can have one when she turns nine and Ellie can't wait. When her Great-aunt Margaret moves into an apartment from a house, she can't take her dog Preston with her. So Ellie will be getting an old boring dog instead of a cute little puppy. Ellie soon realizes that Preston is special, even smart. Maybe, Ellie realizes, she doesn't need a puppy after all.

Shiloh by Phyllis Reynolds Naylor
Atheneum, 1991   GRADES 4–6

When a beagle follows him home in the hills of West Virginia, Marty Preston wants to keep him. But his mom and dad insist that he return the beagle he calls Shiloh to his rightful owner. Unfortunately, the owner, Judd Travers, mistreats both himself and his dogs. When Shiloh comes back to Marty, Marty hides the dog in a pen on his family's property. Not until Shiloh is attacked by a neighboring German shepherd does Marty find a way to keep Shiloh forever. Sequels are *Shiloh Season* and *Saving Shiloh*.

Stay! Keeper's Story by Lois Lowry
Illustrated by True Kelley   Houghton Mifflin, 1997   GRADES 3–4

As he watches his brothers and sister being taken away by people, Keeper hides under some cardboard hoping that no one will see him. Always on his mind is his little sister Whispy, the runt of the litter. Left alone, this poetry reciting canine sets out in the world by himself. First he meets a homeless man who names him Lucky and shares his street life with him. When the homeless man dies, Keeper walks into the life of a photographer who names him Pal. As Pal, Keeper becomes rich and famous. But something is missing and Keeper decides to run away. After roaming the country, Keeper heard the words he was longing to hear, "Can I keep him?"

Strider by Beverly Cleary
Illustrated by Paul O. Zelinsky   Morrow, 1991   GRADES 4–6

See page 82 for a description of this book.

Tornado by Betsy Byars
Illustrated by Doron Ben-Ami   HarperCollins, 1996   GRADES 2–5

When a tornado threatens, Pete the farmhand relates the story of his boyhood with his dog named Tornado. According to Pete, Tornado was found in a doghouse that blew into his yard during a tornado. Pete knew that Tornado belonged to someone else, but that didn't keep him from getting attached to the dog. Tornado, a card-playing, turtle-catching dog was loved by the entire family. When Tornado's original owners claimed him, Pete was devastated until Tornado eventually returned.

33

Where Are Your Horse Stories?

(Picture Books)

Belle's Journey by Marilynn Reynolds
Illustrated by Stephen McCallum   Orca, 1993   GRADES K–3

Every week, Molly rode her old horse Belle to piano lessons. Eight miles to town, and eight miles back, Belle plodded along. Molly was excited when her father suggested selling Belle and buying a new pony. But when Molly and Belle are caught in a blizzard, Molly realizes how much she depends on and loves Belle.

Black Cowboy, Wild Horses: A True Story by Julius Lester
Illustrated by Jerry Pinkney   Dial, 1998   GRADES 2–4

Bob Lemmons, a black cowboy, and his black stallion Warrior track wild mustangs living on the plains. A former slave, Bob Lemmons doesn't know how to read or write but he can track mustangs by just looking at the ground. When Bob comes near the mustangs, he stays very still. He moves only when they move, so they think he is a horse. When a colt dies, it's time for Bob to take over the herd. He leads the horses to a corral with cowboys waiting to close the gate. Bob has done his job.

Custer: The True Story of a Horse by Deborah King
Philomel, 1991   GRADES K–3

Custer is the son of a magnificent horse. But Custer does not aspire to be magnificent. In fact, Custer doesn't even want to be a horse. He'd rather roam the countryside with the cows, doing things that cows like to do. Soon Custer finds himself sold to a riding school. Unfortunately, the cow-loving Custer does not fit in. Once again, Custer is moved, this time to a home by the sea. There he meets a wild gray pony named Minto and

Custer's life changes. Custer the cow-loving horse becomes Custer the magnificent.

The Finest Horse in Town by Jacqueline Briggs Martin
Illustrated by Susan Gaber   HarperCollins, 1992   GRADES K–3

Two sisters own a dry goods store in a small Maine village. They have a smart gray horse named Prince who pulls a shiny black buggy. But who has been taking care of Prince when the sisters were busy with the store? As an old watchmaker recounts, perhaps it was Hooks, a trader, who brought Prince and the buggy to the store. Or maybe it is Sandman Bonney, a man who lost his leg in a logging accident. Or two children, a brother and a sister.

Mrs. Mack by Patricia Polacco
Philomel, 1998   GRADES K–3

In the summer of her tenth year, Patricia Polacco finally is going to get a horse of her own. But when her father takes her to a shabby stable with two rough looking kids, Patricia is devastated. Then comes Mrs. Mack, driving a 1952 Impala and wearing snakeskin boots. With Mrs. Mack's help and understanding, Patricia learns to ride, falling off and getting back on horses. She admires and takes solace in a beautiful copper horse named Penny. Finally, Patricia is able to ride Penny and Penny becomes hers.

No Foal Yet by Jessie Haas
Illustrated by Joseph A. Smith   Greenwillow, 1995   GRADES K–3

Nora can't wait for Bonnie the mare to have her foal. Nora, Gramp, and Gram continuously check on Bonnie but no foal yet. Each afternoon, Nora walks Bonnie around the yard for exercise, and even invites her school class to visit the new foal when it comes. After sleepless nights for both the family and the horse, the foal finally arrives. Nora names the little brown foal Finally!

On the Pampas by Maria Cristina Brusca
Holt, 1991   GRADES K–3

Cristina leaves her home in Buenos Aires to spend the winter vacation on her grandmother's ranch, where her young horse-loving aunt, Susanita, teaches her everything she knows about ranch life. Cristina's story continues in *Mama's Little Ranch on the Pampas* (Holt, 1994) when her mother saves up to buy a ranch of her own.

Seneca by Karen Lee Baker
Greenwillow, 1997   GRADES K–3

> Seneca is a friendly horse with soft brown eyes. When his young owner
> meets him for the first time, she knows that he is the horse for her. She
> visits Seneca everyday after school to feed him his favorite snack, corn
> husks. Every day, she must clean his stall, give him fresh water, and groom
> him. In the fall, they go riding.

Snowy by Berlie Doherty
Illustrated by Keith Bowen   Dial, 1993   GRADES K–3

> Rachel lives in a barge that is pulled by a horse named Snowy. When
> Rachel's class is allowed to bring their pets to class, Rachel wants to bring
> Snowy. But Rachel's teacher, Mrs. Smith, has a secret. The class goes for a
> walk to Rachel's family barge to meet Snowy for themselves.

To the Mountains in the Morning by Diana Wieler
Illustrated by Ange Zhang   Groundwood, 1995   GRADES K–3

> Old Bailey is the gentlest horse at the Rocky Mountain Stables. Almost all
> the horses look up to Old Bailey; she shows them all the tricks of the
> trade. Only Stocking, a beautiful black-and-white stallion, dislikes Old
> Bailey. When a new owner decides to change things, Old Bailey is no
> longer wanted at the stables. So Old Bailey does the only thing she can
> think of, she jumps the fence to freedom with none other than Stocking
> as her companion.

What's the Most Beautiful Thing You Know about Horses?
by Richard Van Camp   Illustrated by George Littlechild
Children's Book Press, 1998   GRADES 1–4

> A young Dogrib Indian boy narrates a poetic story in which he asks fam-
> ily members and friends to name their favorite things about horses. The
> variety of responses he receives offer both personal and cultural insights
> into the animal the Dogrib people call "big dog."

34

Where Are Your Horse Stories?

(Chapter Books)

Beware the Mare by Jessie Haas
Illustrated by Martha Haas   Greenwillow, 1993   GRADES 2–4

When Gramp brings home a new horse, he is a bit skeptical. The horse is called Beware and Gramp wants to make sure there is nothing wrong with it before giving it to Lily. Gramp and Lily go through the motions of putting on a halter, brushing the horse, and even riding it. Beware is no trouble at all. Then one day Lily goes out to greet Beware. The horse almost knocks her over and Lily is frightened at first. But she has no need to be fearful and Lily realizes why the horse is called Beware.

Chico and Dan by Harold Keith
Illustrated by Scott Arbuckle   Eakin, 1998   GRADES 4–6

When Dan Deweese shows up at his great-uncle's ranch, he doesn't know what to expect. He has run away from home and needs a place to work and sleep. Besides, Dan loves horses and can't wait to have one of his own. But his great-uncle Buck Boyce is mean and hard. Dan gets a job milking cows and sleeps with the other hands in the bunkhouse. Dan enjoys his life on the ranch, and when a wild foal is found he nurses the dying foal back to health, names him Chico, and loves him as a friend. But his great-uncle hates wild horses and threatens to turn Chico loose. Only when Dan rescues his great-uncle's beloved horse Jewel does he earn the respect of his great-uncle Buck.

Colt by Nancy Springer
Dial, 1991   GRADES 4–6

Colt has always wanted to ride a horse. But when he enters a riding program, he is stuck with a big and homely horse called Liverwurst. Colt was born with spina bifida and being in a wheelchair is no fun, especially when he has to look up into the face of an ugly giant horse. But when Colt finally gets on Liverwurst, he realizes that it's not too bad. In fact, he wants to do more than just walk with Liverwurst, he wants to trot. Colt's mother has just gotten married and Colt now has a new brother and sister. When the family decides to go riding together, Colt is sure that his family really loves him.

Cougar by Helen Griffith
Greenwillow, 1999   GRADES 4–6

When Nickel sees Cougar, Nickel is positive that the horse is real. But the big black horse actually died in a barn fire a few weeks before. When Pop fixes up a big bike for Nickel, the bike seems to have a mind of its own. In fact, the bike seems to be looking out for Nickel. Could the spirit of Cougar be in the bike?

Gift Horse by Betty Levin
Illustrated by Joseph A. Smith   Greenwillow, 1996   GRADES 4–6

Matt's great-uncle finally keeps his promise and sends him a horse. Matt and his best friend Jerry learn how to take care of Loki, the Norwegian Fjord horse, and realize how much work it is to clean up after a horse. The boys devise a way of making Loki pay for his keep, charging the neighborhood kids for a chance to pet and brush Loki. When Matt enters Loki in a pet show, Loki wins first prize and free food for a year. However, Matt lives in a residential neighborhood where he is not allowed to keep Loki. Matt is sad about having to give up Loki but happy because Loki can now run free.

Horses of Central Park by Michael Slade
Scholastic, 1992   GRADES 4–6

Twelve-year-old Wendell Riley Randolph has always hated his name. His best friend Judith (never-call-me Judy) Henderson is the only one who seems to understand. Every day after school, Wendell goes to Central Park South to talk to the hansom cab horses. When the horses tell Wendell that they are unhappy, Wendell and Judith come up with a plan to free them for a couple of days. With their action plan set, Wendell and Judith sneak into the stable at night and guide the horses to an isolated area of Central Park. The horses promise to return after two days. But worry sets in when the children discover that the missing horses have made front-page news.

I Rode a Horse of Milk White Jade by Diana Lee Wilson
Orchard, 1998   GRADES 5–8

A young girl in fourteenth-century China listens to her grandmother tell about her own girlhood in Mongolia during the time of Kublai Khan. Although she was injured early in her life when her foot was crushed by a horse, young Oyuna grew to love a white mare as much as the rest of her family did; in fact, she felt she could communicate with the horse directly. In order to save the horse's life, Oyuna agreed to dress as a boy and make a long journey on horseback to deliver a package to Kublai Khan himself.

Midnight Rider by Krista Ruepp
Illustrated by Ulrike Heyne   North South, 1995   GRADES 2–4

When Charlie's old horse died, she began visiting the horse Starbright. Starbright's owner, Old Man Grimm, always seems cold and sullen and people stay away from him. Charlie and Starbright, however, soon became friends as Charlie always brings the horse a treat such as a carrot or an apple. But when Charlie asks Old Man Grimm if she can ride Starbright, he tells her to go away. Then one night Charlie decides to ride Starbright without anyone knowing.

More Than a Horse by C. S. Adler
Clarion, 1997   GRADES 5–8

When twelve-year-old Leeann Peters and her mother Rose move from North Carolina to Arizona, Leeann dreads going to her new school and making new friends. To make matters worse, Leeann is not allowed near the horses that she dearly loves. Then Leeann meets Sassy, short for Sassafras, a horse with a mind of its own. Leeann and Sassy develop a bond that even grouchy old Amos admires. Just when Leeann feels that she has finally fit in with the students at her new school and even has a boyfriend, her mother tells her that they will be moving back to North Carolina soon. How can Leeann persuade her mother that Arizona is where she belongs?

35

I Like Reading Stories about School; Do You Have Any?

(Picture Books)

Amazing Grace by Mary Hoffman
Illustrated by Caroline Binch   Dial, 1991   GRADES K–3

Grace loves stories and loves to act, so naturally she's excited when she finds out her class is going to put on the play *Peter Pan.* She's hurt, however, when her classmates tell her she can't play the part of Peter because she's a girl and because she's black. Ma and Nana tell Grace that she can be anything she wants if she puts her mind to it. Grace practices all weekend for the auditions on Monday. When the class votes for the part of Peter, who will get it?

The Awful Aardvarks Go to School by Reeve Lindbergh
Illustrated by Tracy Campbell   Viking, 1997   GRADES K–3

The awful aardvarks go to school and wreak havoc through the alphabet. With rhyming text, they anger the anteater, bully the bunny, and chase the chickens. They are mean and vicious and greedy. They pick on frogs and llamas and a hamster named Tweedy. Finally, they are expelled. And what do they do? They go to the zoo.

The Big Bushy Mustache by Gary Soto
Illustrated by Joe Cepeda   Knopf, 1998   GRADES K–2

As his class gets ready to put on a Cinco de Mayo play, Ricky is excited about the fake mustache he gets to wear because he thinks it makes him look just like his Papi. Then Ricky loses the mustache on his way home from school, but Mama and Papi come up with a perfect solution.

Billy and Belle by Sarah Garland
Viking, 1992   GRADES K–2

Preschooler Belle must accompany her big brother, Billy, to school on the morning her parents go to the hospital for the birth of a new baby. Belle is excited to being going to school in the first place, but it's also pet day, which makes the experience even more exciting for her. She even comes up with her own "pet" to take—a spider!

Chrysanthemum by Kevin Henkes
Greenwillow, 1991   GRADES K–3

Chrysanthemum loves her name; it is absolutely perfect. Until she starts school that is. Everyone laughs at the long name when the teacher calls the roll on the first day of school. The next two days aren't much better. Things change when Chrysanthemum meets her new music teacher, Mrs. Twinkle. The entire class loves Mrs. Twinkle and wants to make a good impression. Not until Mrs. Twinkle reveals her own first name does Chrysanthemum realize that she, indeed, does have an absolutely perfect name.

Froggy Goes to School by Jonathan London
Illustrated by Frank Remkiewicz   Viking, 1996   GRADES K–3

It's the first day of school and Froggy reaches the bus just in time. When he gets on the bus, everyone is laughing at him. He's forgotten his underwear. Then he hears, "Frrrooggyy!" Thank goodness he's been dreaming! Now it's really time for Froggy to get dressed. With flops, zips, zoops, zuts, and zaps, Froggy gets ready for school. Paying attention in school is hard for Froggy until he gets to tell his class about his summer vacation. But Froggy is as forgetful as ever as he leaves his lunch box and baseball cap at school.

Halmoni and the Picnic by Sook Nyul Choi
Illustrated by Karen Dugan   Houghton Mifflin, 1993   GRADES 1–3

Yunmi is worried that her grandmother, newly arrived from Korea, will embarrass her when she comes along on the third-grade class picnic. But contrary to her expectations, Yunmi's classmates are genuinely curious about Halmoni's traditional Korean dress and the special Korean food she has prepared for the occasion.

Hooway for Wodney Wat by Helen Lester
Illustrated by Lynn Munsinger   Houghton Mifflin, 1999   GRADES K–3

Poor Rodney, he was a rodent that couldn't pronounce his *r*'s. So he was known as Wodney Wat. The other rodents teased Wodney, making him the shyest rodent in his elementary school. Wodney was really scared when the biggest, smartest, and meanest rodent Camilla Capybara arrived at school. Then one day, Wodney was chosen to lead the game of Simon Says. All the other rodents knew what Wodney meant when he told them to weed the sign. Everyone except Camilla that is. And when Wodney told everyone to go west, well guess where Camilla went?

Jamaica's Blue Marker by Juanita Havill   Illustrated by
Anne Sibley O'Brien   Houghton Mifflin, 1995   GRADES K–1

Jamaica's teacher asks her to share her markers with Russell. Jamaica doesn't like Russell and when Russell takes her blue marker and ruins Jamaica's picture, she is upset. When Jamaica's teacher tells the class that Russell will be moving, Jamaica doesn't want to make a card for him. Then she realizes how lucky she is for not having to move and gives Russell her blue marker.

Math Curse by Jon Scieszka and Lane Smith
Viking, 1995   GRADES 3–5

When his teacher tells him that almost everything can be thought of as a math problem, a student becomes obsessed with the mathematical problems of everyday life. Getting ready for school becomes a mathematical problem. Classmates' birthdays, the number of classmates, lunch, social studies, and English equations all intrude on this mathematically cursed student's life. When a dream sets him free, he looks forward to a new school day. Until, that is, his teacher tells him that almost everything can be thought of as a science experiment.

Miss Bindergarten Gets Ready for Kindergarten by Joseph Slate
Illustrated by Ashley Wolff   Dutton, 1996   GRADE K

With rhyming text, Miss Bindergarten starts her school day along with her class. While the students are brushing their teeth and combing their hair, Miss Bindergarten is too. While the students pack their bags and backpacks, Miss Bindergarten packs and unpacks her school supplies. While the students walk and ride to school, Miss Bindergarten readies the classroom. Soon, the students have arrived and the classroom is ready for the fun to start.

Miss Malarkey Won't Be In Today by Judy Finchler
Illustrated by Kevin O'Malley   Walker, 1998   GRADES K–3

When Miss Malarkey has a fever and can't go to school, she sits at home and worries about which substitute teacher will take over her class. She fears that the substitute might be Mr. Doberman, who is mean, or Mrs. Ungerware, which sounds like underwear. Or will it be Mr. Lemonjello, who is such a nervous man? Finally, Miss Malarkey can't take it anymore and runs to the school to take care of her students. Everything is fine, until Miss Malarkey starts worrying all over again.

Rachel Parker, Kindergarten Show-off by Ann Martin
Illustrated by Nancy Poydar   Holiday House, 1992   GRADES K–1

Five-year-old Olivia loves her teacher and is the only girl in her kindergarten class who can read. Then one day Rachel Elizabeth Parker moves in next door. They're in the same kindergarten class and soon become friends. But, Rachel can read too and now Rachel gets to read aloud to the class. Jealousy and competitiveness are testing Olivia and Rachel's new friendship. Not until their teacher makes them share reading-aloud duties do they realize that they can help each other and be friends.

Yoko by Rosemary Wells
Hyperion, 1998   GRADES K–3

Yoko's mother fixes Yoko her favorite things for lunch: steamed rice wrapped in seaweed with treasures of cucumber, tuna, and shrimp inside. Unfortunately, the other students laugh at her lunch and her snack of red bean ice cream. When Yoko's teacher comes up with the idea of an international food day, she hopes to create a better understanding of other cultures. Everyone brings in food from all around the world. But no one will touch Yoko's sushi, except for Yoko's new friend Timothy.

36

I Like Reading Stories about School; Do You Have Any?

(Chapter Books)

Amanda Pig, Schoolgirl by Jean Van Leeuwen
Illustrated by Ann Schweninger   Dial, 1997   GRADES 1–2

Amanda is so excited about starting school that she wakes up before the sun does. Amanda will be joining Oliver on the bus so she won't be alone. When she and Oliver take their seats, Amanda sits next to a girl with a lollipop. Amanda introduces herself but the shy girl says nothing, only nodding her head when Amanda asks her if she is scared. So Amanda takes the girl's hand and leads her to school. Amanda loves everything about school. But her shy friend, whom she nicknames Lollipop, won't speak or even smile. Then Amanda comes up with a way to put a smile on her new friend's face.

Andy and Tamika by David A. Adler
Illustrated by Will Hillenbrand   Harcourt, Brace, 1999   GRADES 3–5

Andy has so many things to do and think about. His mother is going to have a baby, so instead of listening to his teacher, Andy spends his time in fourth grade making a list of possible baby names. Andy finds a kitten on the playground, and he will finally have a chance to give away his gerbils at the school carnival. In addition, Andy's friend Tamika will be staying with Andy and his family while her parents recover from an automobile accident. Tamika is worried that she won't feel wanted, especially with a new baby coming. But all is well as Tamika is warmly welcomed into the family.

Darnell Rock, Reporting by Walter Dean Myers
Delacorte, 1994   GRADES 4–7

Thirteen-year-old Darnell Rock is always getting in trouble at school. When the principal at South Oakdale Middle School gives Darnell an ultimatum, Darnell joins the school newspaper in order to get himself out of trouble. Darnell's not sure if this newspaper idea is a good one, but gets interested when he decides to write a story about Sweeby, a homeless man who was in Vietnam with his dad. When his initial attempt to interview Sweeby fails, Darnell realizes that it takes more than sympathy and handouts to restore a person's dignity.

Eagle Song by Joseph Bruchac
Illustrated by Dan Andreasen   Dial, 1997   GRADES 3–5

When Danny Bigtree moves from a Mohawk reservation to New York City, he must find a way to withstand the teasing of his fourth-grade classmates, with some help from his mom and dad. Danny's story will ring true with anyone who has been the new kid in school or has moved from a rural to an urban setting.

Frindle by Andrew Clements
Illustrated by Brian Selznick   Simon and Schuster, 1996   GRADES 3–5

See page 5 for a description of this book.

Hey, New Kid by Betsy Duffey
Illustrated by Ellen Thompson   Viking, 1996   GRADES 2–4

Cody's family has just moved from Topeka. The thought of starting a new school without his best friends Aaron and Kate makes Cody feel insecure. To impress his new classmates, Cody invents a new image, a superduper Cody. When superduper skater Cody is invited to a skating party, his lies are exposed when he ends up on skates in the girls' bathroom. Cody soon realizes that one doesn't have to have cool parents or come from Alaska or be a genius to be liked by his new classmates.

Horrible Harry Moves Up to Third Grade by Suzy Kline
Illustrated by Frank Remkiewicz   Viking, 1998   GRADES 2–4

Harry and his friend Doug are ready to start third grade. When they finally find their third grade classroom, they are relieved to find their same old teacher Miss Mackle and Song Lee, but unfortunately Harry's enemy Sidney is there too. When the class goes on a field trip to a mine, everyone but Harry is ecstatic. Tension mounts between Harry and Sidney when Sidney teases Harry about his fear of being underground. Finally, Harry gets the last laugh when he tricks Sidney. But when Sidney is missing, Harry is worried that something bad has happened. Harry soon realizes that Sidney is as much a part of his life as Miss Mackle.

Joshua T. Bates in Trouble Again by Susan Shreve
Illustrated by Roberta Smith   Knopf, 1997   GRADES 3–5

It's the week after Thanksgiving and Joshua has finally been promoted to the fourth grade. But he needs to act and look different or he won't fit in with his fourth grade classmates. Joshua goes to school in his father's shirt, combing his hair to stand straight up like the most popular kid in class, Tommy Wilhelm. Not until Joshua stands up to Tommy Wilhelm and his friends does he realize that he doesn't have to impress anyone to enjoy the fourth grade.

Louise Takes Charge by Stephen Krensky
Illustrated by Susanna Natti   Dial, 1998   GRADES 2–4

When Louise returns to school in the fall, everything seems normal except Jasper, who has grown over the summer and has become the new class bully. Jasper does not hesitate to steal lunches, copy notes, and boss his classmates around. Louise comes up with a plan to deal with Jasper's bullying. First, Louise becomes Jasper's apprentice and eventually the entire class is working for Jasper. When Jasper decides to fire his apprentices, he realizes that he can't bully them around any more. They are a team now and stick together to put Jasper in his place.

Maizon at Blue Hill by Jacqueline Woodson
Delacorte, 1992   GRADES 4–6

Maizon accepts a scholarship to an exclusive private boarding school and finds that she is one of only five African-American students there. While the school offers excellent academic opportunities for her, she must also confront racism and stereotypes before she can begin to feel at home in this new setting.

Mayfield Crossing by Vaunda Micheaux Nelson
Illustrated by Leonard Jenkins   Putnam, 1993   GRADES 4–6

See page 96 for a description of this book.

My Name Is María Isabel by Alma Flor Ada   Illustrated by
Kathryn Dyble Thompson   Atheneum, 1993   GRADES 2–4

María Isabel Salazar López is proud of her name and her Puerto Rican heritage, so she finds it especially difficult when her teacher insists on calling her Mary Lopez, but she's too shy to speak up for herself. And as if that's not enough, her mom has just taken a new job so she's no longer at home when María Isabel gets home from school in the afternoon. She eventually manages to figure out a way to find her own voice in school.

Re-elect Nutty by Dean Hughes
Atheneum, 1995   GRADES 4–6

Nutty's presidency last year was horrible. Now he is running again, this time as an honest candidate. But someone is sabotaging his campaign. Nutty blames Mindy, the opposition, and things get really dirty. With the help of his friends, Nutty plans his next move. When his plans backfire, Nutty finds out who has been sabotaging his campaign. Confused and hurt, Nutty decides to withdraw from the campaign. But honesty does pay off as Nutty not only wins the presidency but also learns a lesson about friendship.

Starting School by Johanna Hurwitz
Illustrated by Karen Dugan   Morrow, 1998   GRADES 3–5

Marius and Marcus are twins and little brothers of Lucas Cott, the class clown. When the twins start kindergarten, teachers dread the thought of having them in their class. Thank goodness they have been assigned to separate classrooms. When Lucas tells Marius that there was a mouse in Mrs. Greenstein's room, he is obsessed with finding the mouse. When Lucas teaches Marcus how to play 52 pickup, Marcus has to show his class. To prove who has the worse twin, the teachers decide to trade classes, not knowing that the boys have decided to trade identities to find out who has the better teacher. Thinking they have each other's twin, the teachers are glad to get back to their own classes.

The View from Saturday by E. L. Konigsburg
Atheneum, 1996   GRADES 4–7

No sixth grade Academic Bowl team has ever beaten an eighth grade team, not at Ephipany Middle School or any school in the state of New York. But Mrs. Olinski's team does. Mrs. Olinski, returning to teaching after an automobile accident that left her a paraplegic, slowly makes her choices for the Academic Bowl. In flashbacks, E. L. Konigsburg invites us to meet Noah, Nadia, Ethan and Julian. The foursome, who call themselves the "Souls," meets every Saturday at four o'clock for tea. And it is no surprise to Mrs. Olinski when she finds out their name and realizes their ability to work together and respect one another as a team and as individuals.

37
I Need Help
on a Science Project

Awesome Experiments in Force and Motion by Michael DiSpezio
Illustrated by Catherine Leary   Sterling, 1998   GRADES 4–6

There are over sixty experiments, each including a list of materials needed, what to do, the science behind the experiment, and some interesting facts about the experiment. Includes line illustrations and an index.

Don't Try This at Home! Science Fun for Kids on the Go
by Vicki Cobb and Kathy Darling   Illustrated by
True Kelley   Morrow, 1998   GRADES 3–5

More than sixty safe experiments to perform outside and with everyday things. From learning to crack the code on license plates to measuring g-force on a roller coaster, these experiments help students discover the world around them. The book is divided according to places such as school or beach. Place and subject indexes are included.

Janice VanCleave's Constellations for Every Kid
Wiley, 1997   GRADES 4–6

This book describes over twenty constellations and includes directions on how to find them in the sky. Each chapter contains background information and questions and answers. Of course, science activities are included with each. The book includes star maps, a list of the constellations, a list of the stars, a glossary of terms, and an index.

Optics Book: Fun Experiments with Light, Vision and Color
by Shar Levine and Leslie Johnstone   Illustrated by
Jason Coons   Sterling, 1998   GRADES 4–6

Properties of light and color are explored in this book of more than thirty-five experiments. Subjects include the speed of light, refraction, and optical instruments. Each experiment includes a list of materials, what to do, and what happened. Containing a glossary and index, this book is illustrated with line drawings and pictures.

Physics Lab in the Home by Bob Friedhoffer
Illustrated by Joe Hosking   Franklin Watts, 1997   GRADES 4–6

Using everyday home appliances and objects, students can learn the history of plumbing and how it works and how refrigerators work and why we need them. Each experiment includes a list of materials, a caution, and the results. Also included are a glossary, a list of resources, a basic review of scientific principles, and an index.

Shocking, Slimy, Stinky, Shiny Science Experiments
by Steve Parker   Sterling, 1998   GRADES 2–4

Containing more than ninety experiments dealing with light, electricity, slime, and sense of smell, this book shows students how to perform activities as diverse as making an electromagnet and smelling with one's mouth. Each chapter is introduced with background information. Dispersed throughout the experiments are snippets of information on bright ideas of history, such as the first person to study electricity. Includes a glossary of terms and an index.

Universe: The Hands-on Approach to Science
by Andrew Haslam   Thomson Learning, 1995   GRADES 4–6

Demonstrating how the universe works, the book contains science experiments on day and night, seasons, the solar system, and living in space. Each experiment includes a list of materials and instructions for performing the experiment. The book includes a glossary and index.

What Makes a Magnet? by Franklyn Branley
Illustrated by True Kelley   HarperCollins, 1996   GRADES K–3

Describing how magnets work, this book contains activities to perform including how to prove that the whole world is a magnet. Simple text and playful illustrations are good for lower elementary school students.

38

Do You Have Any Books Written Like a Diary?

Amelia Takes Command by Marissa Moss
Tricycle, 1998   GRADES 4–6

As with the other *Amelia* titles, Amelia writes about her life in her notebook. Amelia is now in the fifth grade and is miserable. She doesn't like her teacher, her best friend Leah is in a different class and befriending other girls, and Hilary, the class bully, calls her names and makes fun of her. Then Nadia invites her to Space Camp where Amelia is picked as commander of her space team. Although a hero in space camp, Amelia must return to school to face Hilary. Will Amelia be brave enough to stand up to Hilary?

Birdie's Lighthouse by Deborah Hopkinson
Illustrated by Kimberly Bulcken Root   Atheneum, 1997   GRADES K–5

On her tenth birthday, Birdie receives a diary and she records her life in a coastal Maine town. Then her father is sent to Turtle Island to be the lightkeeper and Birdie must leave her friends and spend a solitary life with her family. When her brother Nate leaves the little island to join the crew of a fishing boat, Birdie must be the one to assist her father. Her father teaches her how to keep the light and Birdie is soon taking the midnight shift. When Birdie's papa takes sick, it's up to Birdie to keep the light burning during a storm and guide a fishing boat to safety.

Diary of a Drummer Boy by Marlene Targ Brill
Illustrated by Michael Garland   Millbrook 1998   GRADES 3–5

In December 1860, Orian Perseus Howe turns twelve and receives a diary from his father to write down thoughts best kept to himself. His father played the fife in the Mexican War and both Orian and his younger brother Lyston play the drum. When talk of a war between the states spreads, the boys and their father play to crowds at nightly war meetings. Then, in 1861, Lyston and his father enlist in the Union Army. Soon afterwards, Orian enlists as a drummer boy. Orian, Lyston, and their father experience firsthand the horrors of war.

Diary of a Monster's Son by Ellen Conford
Illustrated by Tom Newsom   Little, Brown, 1999   GRADES 3–5

Bradley Fentriss looks like an ordinary boy. But his dad is not your ordinary dad. Bradley's dad is really big and hairy and he has fangs. In his diary, Bradley relates the daily events of living with a monster dad. Heads turn when Bradley's dad shops with Bradley for new school clothes, goes to the Parent-Teacher Night, and goes trick-or-treating at Halloween. But best of all, Bradley's dad is fun and when they have a picnic in the snow, everybody realizes that monster or not, Bradley's dad is just a dad.

The Great Green Notebook of Katie Roberts: Who Just Turned Twelve on Monday by Amy Hest   Illustrated by
Sonja Lamut   Candlewick, 1998   GRADES 4–6

In this continuation of *Love You, Soldier* and *The Private Notebook of Katie Roberts, Age 11*, Katie receives another diary from Mrs. Leitstein on her twelfth birthday. Katie is now in the seventh grade. She deals with jealousy when Joyce threatens to take her best friend Lucie away from her. She discovers boys, lipstick, and her first dance. Then her mother is hit by a truck and Katie writes to Mrs. Leitstein for help. When Mrs. Leitstein arrives, she is more than a comfort for Katie.

I Thought My Soul Would Rise and Fly: The Diary of Patsy, a Freed Girl by Joyce Hansen   Scholastic, 1997   GRADES 4–6

At the end of the Civil War, Patsy is left with no family and no place to go. She continues living for a while in the home of her old Master, secretly learning to read and write by listening in on the Master's children's school lessons. She continues with her day-to-day labor, looking forward to the promised opening of a new school she will be allowed to attend.

Jorah's Journal by Judith Caseley
Greenwillow, 1997   GRADES 2–4

When Jorah's family moves, she has to attend a new school. Her mother gives her a journal as a housewarming gift and Jorah finds nothing good to write in it. Her new classmates make fun of her green shoes. A boy named Jay pulls her hair, and she and her little brother Caleb like their old world better. Jorah brings cupcakes to school for her birthday, but still feels that she has no friends. Then the doorbell rings and Mora, a girl from her class brings her a birthday present. Finally, her new world is good.

The Journal of Wong Ming-Chung: A Chinese Miner
by Laurence Yep   Scholastic, 2000   GRADES 3–5

Eleven-year-old Wong Ming-Chung, nicknamed Runt, begins his journal in 1851, shortly after his uncle leaves China for the gold fields of America. Runt joins him soon afterward in order to escape the war and poverty at home, but finds that life in America is also difficult, far from the Golden Mountain he was expecting. He works alongside his uncle in the mining camp, eking out a living in a harsh new land that still holds the promise of a better life.

My Worst Days Diary by Suzanne Altman
Illustrated by Diane Allison   Bantam, 1994   GRADES 2–3

Maureen "Mo" Murphy decides to keep a diary when awful things begin to happen to her. On the first day of her new school, Mo burps in front of the class. As the days pass she accidentally gives her teacher the wrong letter, arrives at a classmate's party a day early, steps in dog doo, and gets toilet paper stuck on the bottom of her shoe. Then Mo realizes that the kids like her after all and begins keeping a diary of her greatest days.

Picture of Freedom: The Diary of Clotee, a Slave Girl
by Patricia McKissack   Scholastic   GRADES 5–7

Clotee is no ordinary slave; she can read and write. One of Clotee's many duties in the big house is to fan William, the son of Mas' Henley and Miz Lilly, when the weather is hot. While William is being taught his lessons, Clotee pays attention and learns too. She secretly devours old newspapers and books, continually learning new words and meanings, and writes in her diary whenever she gets a chance. When a tutor, Mr. Harms, arrives from Washington, D.C., Clotee fears that he will find her out. But Mr. Harms has a secret too. He is a conductor on the Underground Railroad. As the cruelty of her life continues, Clotee is given the chance to escape. Will she take it? A book in the Dear America series.

Running Girl by Sharon Bell Mathis

Browndeer/Harcourt, Brace, 1997 GRADES 3–5

See page 52 for a description of this book.

Willow Chase, Kansas Territory, 1847 by Kathleen Duey

Aladdin, 1997 GRADES 4–6

Willow is given a diary by her aunt to record the events of her family's journey with the wagon train heading for California. After her father drowns, her mother remarries a man she calls Mr. Hansen, for he can never replace her real father. Life on the trail is rough, a lot rougher than Willow could have ever imagined. When Willow and her dog Fancy are knocked into the river, everyone assumes that she drowned just like her father. But Willow and Fancy survive with the help of an Indian and find their way back to the wagon train. Number 5 in the American Diaries series.

39

Do You Have Any Good Books for Kindergartners?

The Bat in the Boot by Annie Cannon
Orchard, 1996

> See page 99 for a description of this book.

The Big Green Pocketbook by Candice Ranson   Illustrated by
Felicia Bond   Laura Geringer, 1993

> A girl and her mom take the bus to town to take care of several errands.
> Along the way she collects many things: ticket stubs from the bus, lollipops
> at the bank, a calendar at the dry cleaners, and a key chain from the bank.
> She keeps all her treasures in the big green pocketbook that her mother
> gave her. She's sleepy by the time they return home and suddenly realizes
> she does not have her big green pocketbook with her. Where can it be?

Bootsie Barker Bites by Barbara Bottner   Illustrated by
Peggy Rathmann   Putnam, 1992

> Bootsie Barker's mother is best friends with the mother of a young girl
> who must play with Bootsie no matter how horrible Bootsie is. The girl
> dreads Bootsie's visits, especially when Bootsie pretends to be a girl-eat-
> ing dinosaur. As the girl dreams that Bootsie and her mother will move
> away, Bootsie comes to stay overnight while her parents visit Chicago.
> After undergoing Bootsie's torments, the young girl finally decides to take
> matters into her own hands and pretends to be a paleontologist hunting
> for dinosaur bones.

Chrysanthemum by Kevin Henkes
Greenwillow, 1991

> See page 127 for a description of this book.

Elizabeti's Doll by Stephanie Stuve-Bodeen. Illustrated by Christy Hale
Lee & Low, 1998

> After her mother has a new baby, little Elizabeti wants a baby of her own to care for, so she adopts a large rock. Imitating all the actions of her mother, Elizabeti finds her rock much more agreeable than her baby brother until one day the rock disappears. Where can it have gone? A charming and amusing story set in Tanzania.

Grandpa Toad's Secrets by Keiko Kasza
Putnam, 1995

> As Grandpa and Little Toad walk, Grandpa shares his secrets for staying clear of hungry enemies. Grandpa also gets the chance to demonstrate how to be brave and how to be smart by scaring a snake and tricking a snapping turtle. But when Grandpa and Little Toad face a huge hairy monster, Grandpa loses his courage. So Little Toad goes into action, being both brave and smart.

Horace and Morris but Mostly Dolores by James Howe
Illustrated by Amy Walrod   Atheneum, 1999

> Horace, Morris, and Dolores are friends. They love adventure and they have always done everything together. Then one day, Horace and Morris decide that "a boy mouse must do what a boy mouse must do." They join the Mega-Mice, a no-girls-allowed club. Dolores is at first downhearted, but then she decides that "a girl must do what a girl must do" and she knocks on the door of the Cheese Puffs clubhouse. Horace, Morris, and Dolores miss playing with each other but they are sure that their friendship has changed. Until one day, a bored Dolores and Chloris build a clubhouse of their own with, of course, Horace and Morris and Boris.

I Had a Hippopotamus by Hector Viveros Lee
Lee & Low, 1996

> While eating from a box of *galletas* (animal crackers), a young boy imagines that each cracker is a live animal that he gives as a gift to various family members and friends. A playful patterned text makes this a perfect story for young children who are getting ready to read.

Jonathan and His Mommy by Irene Smalls-Hector
Illustrated by Michael Hays   Little, Brown, 1992

> Jonathan and his mom take a walk down their city street but not in the usual way. They zigzag, hop, dance, and even walk backwards before they find their way home again.

Louella Mae, She's Run Away by Karen Alarcón
Illustrated by Rosanne Litzinger   Holt, 1997

> Where can Louella Mae be? This text in rhyme follows the hunt for the elusive Louella Mae. Is she in the cornfield, the hay? Where oh where is Louella Mae? Everyone frantically searches the stream, the tree, in the barn, everywhere. Eventually, Louella Mae is found, sleeping . . . without a sound.

Max Found Two Sticks by Brian Pinkney
Simon & Schuster, 1994

> Brooding Max isn't in the mood to talk to anyone. He'd rather just sit on his front porch and pout. But when he notices that two sticks on the ground make perfect drumsticks, he begins to communicate with neighbors passing by thumping out his feelings, and he manages to drum his bad mood away completely.

Miss Spider's Tea Party by David Kirk
Scholastic, 1994

> Lonely Miss Spider would love nothing more than to have friends over for tea, but all the bugs turn down her invitations because they think she really wants to eat them. Only after she showers her kindness on a rain-soaked moth do the other bugs accept her gracious offer, and a lovely time is had by all.

New Shoes for Silvia by Johanna Hurwitz
Illustrated by Jerry Pinkney   Morrow, 1993

> In South America, Silvia receives a wonderful present from Tia Rosita— a new pair of red shoes! The shoes are too big though, and Silvia is disappointed when mama says they will have to be put away until Silvia's feet grow big enough to fit them. As each week passes, Silvia tries on the shoes again and again hoping that they will fit. When will she be big enough to wear her new red shoes?

Old Black Fly by Jim Aylesworth
Illustrated by Stephen Gammell   Holt, 1992

> An old black fly leads us through the alphabet in this fun, rhyming text. With the refrain of "Shoo fly!, Shoo fly!, Shooo!" he coughs on cookies, steals jelly, pesters the parrot, and sleeps on a stack of clean underwear. Then the old black fly makes his first and last mistake; he lands on mama's table and snoozes, *zzzz*. SMACK!

Outside Inn by George Ella Lyon
Illustrated by Vera Rosenberry   Orchard, 1991

> Four children play in the mud and dirt, pretending to fix meals using the ingredients at hand. Puddle ink to drink, gravel crunch for lunch, and worms and dirt for dessert are among the food offered at the Outside Inn.

Pete's a Pizza by William Steig
HarperCollins, 1998

> See page 3 for a description of this book.

Pigs Ahoy! by David McPhail
Dutton, 1995

> A rollicking, rhyming story of an ocean cruise overrun by pigs. The pigs cause chaos on every part of the ship; they paint the boiler room, have a food fight in the dining hall, and irritate the captain. When the captain has had enough, the pigs are removed from the ship. One passenger finds, however, that things are just too quiet and more than a little bit boring without the pigs around.

Rachel Parker, Kindgarten Show-off by Ann Martin
Illustrated by Nancy Poydar   Holiday House, 1992

> See page 129 for a description of this book.

Round Is a Mooncake by Roseanne Thong
Illustrated by Grace Lin   Chronicle, 2000

> Basic shapes (circle, square, rectangle) are found in everyday objects in a Chinese-American girl's neighborhood in a rhyming story that combines specific cultural items such as rice bowls and dim sum with universal items such as the moon.

That's Good! That's Bad! by Margery Cuyler
Illustrated by David Catrow　Henry Holt, 1991

> When a boy gets a red balloon at the zoo, it lifts him high into the sky. Oh that's good. No that's bad. It's just the beginning of his adventures as he meets a scary snake, a giraffe, and a lion snoring in the grass. How will he ever find his way back to his parents?

Watch Out! Big Bro's Coming! by Jez Alborough
Candlewick, 1997

> Panic ensues when a little mouse tells a frog, the frog tells a parrot, the parrot tells a chimpanzee, and the chimpanzee tells an elephant that Big Bro's coming. Big Bro is rough and tough and everyone knows how big Big Bro is. When no one is brave enough to check on the whereabouts of Big Bro, the little mouse volunteers to investigate. Then Big Bro comes and everyone covers his or her eyes. Everyone, except the mouse, who is the only one knows Big Bro's identity. Big Bro is rough and tough, but is he really big?

You're the Boss, Baby Duck by Amy Hest
Illustrated by Jill Barton　Candlewick, 1997

> When a new baby arrives in the house, everyone is happy about it except Baby Duck. Grampa understands how Baby Duck feels, though, and helps her realize how important being a big sister can be.

Yours Truly, Goldilocks by Alma Flor Ada
Illustrated by Leslie Tryon　Atheneum, 1998

> Told in letters, this story is the sequel to *Dear Peter Rabbit*. The three pigs are finally in their brick house and Peter Rabbit and Mr. McGregor have become friends. The three pigs invite everyone to a housewarming party and invitations are sent to Little Red Riding Hood, Peter Rabbit, Goldilocks, and Baby Bear. Letters are written between friends and plans are made. Unfortunately, Wolfy Lupus and Fer O'Cious, two big bad wolves, plan to spoil the fun. Will the wolves succeed or will they end up needing the services of Speedy Raccoon again?

40

Do You Have Any Good
Books for First Graders?

Abuela by Arthur Dorros   Illustrated by Elisa Kleven   Dutton, 1991

Rosalba's grandmother speaks Spanish. With Rosalba explaining the Spanish words and phrases of her grandmother, they go by bus to visit the park. They imagine the wonderful things they could see if they could be like birds and fly all over the city. Includes a glossary of Spanish words.

Coyote Steals the Blanket: A Ute Tale retold and illustrated by
Janet Stevens   Holiday House, 1993

That coyote! He's always getting into trouble. Hummingbird tells him not to touch those blankets, but he does and now look what's happened. Coyote is being chased by a giant rock! Who can help him escape from the rock? Not anyone you'd expect!

Dear Juno by Soyung Pak   Illustrated by Susan K. Hartung   Viking, 1999

Juno looks forward to the letters he receives from his grandmother back in Korea and he enjoys responding to them. Even though Juno and his grandmother speak different languages, they always find ways to communicate with each other through the pictures, pressed flowers, and leaves they send to each other.

Fox on Stage by James Marshall   Dial, 1993

Fox is up to his usual silliness. In the first chapter, Grannie fox breaks her legs and has to go to the hospital and Fox tries to cheer her up. In the second chapter, Fox and his friends go to a magic show. When the magician hears Fox complaining, he shows Fox a trick that takes away all of Fox's doubt. In the third chapter, Fox and his friends put on a play. When everything goes wrong, it turns out all right as the audience thinks Fox is being humorous.

The Golly Sisters Ride Again by Betsy Byars
Illustrated by Sue Truesdell   HarperCollins, 1994

The Golly sisters, May May and Rose share their adventures in five stories. Is a goat bad luck? Rose thinks so and she won't perform until someone removes the goat. Sure enough, Rose is right, as the goat causes chaos
in the first chapter. The second chapter has the Golly sisters visiting a
talking rock. Next, they have an argument over who is to be the princess
and who is to be the troll. The fourth chapter has the Golly sisters taking
a Golly holiday, otherwise known as Golliday. Finally, the Golly sisters
weather a storm as best they can: hiding under the bed and singing as
loud as possible.

Henry and Mudge and the Bedtime Thumps by Cynthia Rylant
Illustrated by Suçie Stevenson   Bradbury, 1991

Henry and his dog Mudge are visiting his grandmother in the country.
Henry's grandmother has never met Mudge and Henry is afraid that
Mudge might have to sleep outside. When Mudge knocks over a pink
flamingo, a wishing well, and a bowl of peppermints, Henry's worries
come to pass as Mudge is put outside. How will Henry sleep without
Mudge? How will Mudge sleep without Henry?

Lily's Purple Plastic Purse by Kevin Henkes
Greenwillow, 1996

Lily loves everything about school, especially her teacher, Mr. Slinger.
One day Lily brings her new shiny purple purse to school to show everyone. She is very excited and can't wait to demonstrate how her purse plays
a tune when it is opened. Because she is disobeying, Mr. Slinger takes the
purse away from Lily. Lily gets very angry and says a mean thing to Mr.
Slinger. Later when she gets home, she feels very sorry that she said the
mean thing. Will Mr. Slinger forgive her?

Little Red Cowboy Hat by Susan Lowell
Illustrated by Randy Cecil   Henry Holt, 1997

Little Red lives out West. She has red, red hair and a red cowboy hat. Her
mom sends her to check on her grandmother, who is not feeling well.
Along the way, Little Red encounters a suspicious looking stranger, but
Grandma comes to the rescue. Little Red learns that a girl has to stick up
for herself.

Mac and Marie and the Train Toss Surprise
by Elizabeth Fitzgerald Howard
Illustrated by Gail Gordon Carter   Four Winds, 1993

Mac the train enthusiast knows the exact time all the trains pass by their house in Baltimore. He hopes to be a train engineer one day himself. His Uncle Clem works as a Pullman porter, and Mac even knows which of the passing trains he will be on. As the train comes north from Florida, Uncle Clem has promised to toss Mac and his sister Marie a special surprise from the moving train. Anticipation builds while Mac and Marie wait for the train: what will the surprise be?

Martha Speaks by Susan Meddaugh
Houghton Mifflin, 1992

See page 113 for a description of this book.

Nate the Great and the Stolen Base by Marjorie Sharmat
Illustrated by Marc Simont   Dial, 1992

Nate the Great is not only a detective, he is a baseball player. When Oliver's second base, an octopus, is missing, Nate the Great is on the case. Nate and Oliver go to Oliver's house to investigate. Then they go outside to search for clues. But the clues lead them back to Oliver's house. Will Nate the Great solve the case?

Peeping Beauty by Mary Jane Auch
Holiday House, 1993

Poulette dreams of becoming a famous ballerina. The other chickens scoff at her plans and warn her to stay away from the talent scout from New York City. The talent scout, who happens to be a fox, tells Poulette that he is hiring dancers for a ballet called *Peeping Beauty*. When Poulette finds herself the main course instead of the main dancer, she goes into action. With her muscles strong and hard from hours of practice, Poulette jetés across the stage and, with the help of her friends, floors the fox.

Piggie Pie! by Margie Palatini
Illustrated by Howard Fine   Clarion, 1995

Gritch the Witch wakes up grumpy and very hungry for some delicious piggie pie! She needs eight plump pigs for her recipe, so she flies right over to old MacDonald's farm. Funny though, when she gets there, she does not see any pigs anywhere—only some funny-looking ducks, some lumpy cows, and some very fat chickens.

Saving Sweetness by Diane Stanley
Illustrated by G. Brian Karas   Putnam, 1996

> When Sweetness runs away from the orphanage, the sheriff sets out to retrieve her. This doesn't turn out to be easy, though, since Sweetness refuses to go back to the orphanage and mean old Mrs. Sump. Before Sweetness and the sheriff return to town, they capture the outlaw Coyote Pete, and Sweetness finds a new home for herself and all the other orphans.

Stellaluna by Janell Cannon
Harcourt, Brace, 1993

> Mother Bat and her soft new baby fly through the forest until an owl attacks, and the two are separated. Alone and scared, Stellaluna clings to a branch and eventually falls into a bird's nest. She tries very hard to fit in with her new family but cannot help feeling very different from the birds. One night, she meets others of her kind and discovers how wonderful it is to be a bat.

Trick or Treat, Smell My Feet by Diane De Groat
Morrow, 1998

> Gilbert's little sister Lola wants to do everything he does. But she's not old enough to go to school and has to stay home and be a ballerina for Halloween. Gilbert wants to be the only Captain Zigg in his class and is disappointed when he sees other boys with the same costume. But Gilbert is in for a surprise. Instead of bringing his Captain Zigg costume, he's brought Lola's ballerina costume by accident. He puts on Lola's costume in hopes of switching with her during the school parade. But Lola's too slow and they have nowhere to change. What is Gilbert to do?

Zelda and Ivy by Laura McGee Kvasnosky
Illustrated by Laura McGee   Candlewick, 1998

> Zelda and Ivy are sisters. In three short stories, Zelda and Ivy test their trust in one another as Zelda, the oldest, conjures up daring schemes for her little sister Ivy. In the first story, Ivy is designated the fabulous fox on the flying trapeze. Zelda, of course, is the announcer. In the next story, Zelda decides to paint Ivy's tail blue. In the final story, Zelda has a baton and Ivy wants a baton. When Zelda tells Ivy to put crayon bits under her pillow and wish for a baton, Ivy can't wait. Ivy's wish comes true, but she soon realizes that it's Zelda's baton and she must learn a lesson about sharing.

41

Do You Have Any Good Books for Second Graders?

Alison's Fierce and Ugly Halloween by Marion Dane Bauer
Illustrated by Laurie Spencer   Hyperion, 1997

> Alison loves Halloween. One year she was a ballerina, then a fairy princess. But this year Alison wants to be a fierce, ugly pirate. So Alison and her friend Cindy put on eye patches and scars and pretend to be mean pirates. When their fierce and ugly costumes don't elicit a fearful response, Alison is disappointed. She throws pebbles at a neighbor's house in anger. Her anger soon changes to guilt and Alison confesses her crime.

Amazing Grace by Mary Hoffman
Illustrated by Caroline Binch   Dial, 1991

> See page 126 for a description of this book.

Aunt Harriet's Underground Railroad in the Sky by Faith Ringgold
Crown, 1992

> Cassie and her brother, BeBe, take a pretend flight in the sky where BeBe hops right on Aunt Harriet's railroad. Cassie has to seek advice from Aunt Harriet and retrace the steps of those who escaped to freedom on the Underground Railroad long ago to find BeBe again.

The Bunyans by Audrey Wood
Illustrated by David Shannon   Blue Sky, 1996

> When Paul Bunyan meets Carrie McIntie, it is love at first sight. They are married in an enormous crystal chamber, and after the ceremony some folks call it Mammoth Cave. Soon the Bunyans have children, a boy named Little Jean and a girl named Teeny. The family's adventures are responsible for creating many natural wonders including Niagara Falls

and Bryce Canyon. As the country grows up, so do the children, and they leave home leaving Paul and Carrie to retire to the wilderness.

Chibi: A True Story from Japan by Barbara Brenner and Julia Takaya
Illustrated by June Otani   Clarion, 1996

All the residents of Tokyo got caught up several years ago in the drama of a mother duck who laid her eggs and raised her ducklings in the middle of a busy business section in the center of the city. News photographer Mr. Sato named the smallest duckling "Chibi" and tracked the ducks' progress daily. When a typhoon hit and the ducks seemed to disappear, everyone waited for days to learn the fate of Chibi and his family.

How the Second Grade Got $8,205.50 to Visit the Statue of Liberty
by Nathan Zimelman   Illustrated by Bill Slavin   Albert Whitman, 1992

How did the second grade get $8,205.50? Well, it wasn't from the paper drive, because they had to pay back the recycler. It wasn't from the lemonade stand, as Eleanor's cat fell into the tub of lemonade. It wasn't from babysitting or dog walking. No parent was willing to let them baby-sit. It wasn't from the candy sales; they only made $7.50. The car wash proves to be the most profitable. That is, of course, after two thieves who were making their getaway at the wrong time have been captured.

Mailing May by Michael O. Tunnel   Illustrated by Ted Rand
Greenwillow, 1997

May wants to visit her Grandma Mary, but the family cannot afford a train ticket. Things seem hopeless until Pa comes up with a plan. With help from Ma's cousin Leonard, Pa convinces the postmaster to send May on the mail car classified as a baby chick! May does indeed ride in the mail car and makes her way over the mountains to visit her Grandma. Based on a true story.

Man Out at First by Matt Christopher
Illustrated by Ellen Beier   Little, Brown, 1993

When Theodore, a.k.a. Turtleneck Jones, gets hit in the chest with a baseball, he has second thoughts about playing the game. Turtleneck is ashamed because he blacked out when he was hit and now he flinches every time someone throws a ball at him. And to make matters worse, his coach is replacing him at first base. When his blind neighbor, Mr. Shaw, asks Turtleneck to help mend his porch, Turtleneck ignores him and goes to his room. When Mr. Shaw comes over and talks to Turtleneck,

Turtleneck feels a lot better. The next day and with Mr. Shaw in the crowd, Turtleneck is finally put back into the baseball game and regains his confidence.

Mary Marony Hides Out by Suzy Kline
Illustrated by Blanche Sims   Putnam, 1993

> Mary Marony can't wait. Her favorite author, Jan Berry, is visiting her school and she wants an autographed copy of the author's latest book. When the author asks the students in the auditorium who has read her new book, Mary Marony hesitantly raises her hand. But Jan Berry asks Mary to stand up and then asks Mary her name. Slowly, Mary stutters out her name to the giggles of other classmates and her own embarrassment. At recess, Mary hides in the bathroom. Her friends soon find her and the three of them eavesdrop on other girls' conversations. When a third grader confronts them, Mary learns a new word . . . *nincompoop*. Soon this new word lands Mary the winner of a class spelling contest and the prize of having lunch with the author.

Morning on the Lake by Barbara Waboose
Illustrated by Karen Reczuch   Kids Can, 1998

> When a young Ojibway boy spends the day on the lake with his *mishomis* (grandfather), they both claim morning, afternoon, and night as their favorite time of day. In the morning from their birchbark canoe on the lake they see a loon, in the afternoon as they're hiking up a hill, they see an eagle, and at night, walking through the forest, they see a pack of wolves. Initially the boy is just a little bit fearful of each animal until his *mishomis* places each one in its cultural context for him.

My Brother, Ant by Betsy Byars   Illustrated by Marc Simont   Viking, 1997

> Ant's big brother tells four stories about his pesky little brother. First he has to chase monsters out from under Ant's bed, then Ant draws on his homework. Later Ant wants to hear a story, and finally he needs help writing a letter to Santa Claus.

Onion Sundaes by David A. Adler
Illustrated by Heather Harms Maione   Random, 1994

> Herman Foster is a magician. In fact, he likes to be called Houdini. When Houdini shows his cousin Janet his onion sundae trick, they decide to go to the grocery store for more supplies so Houdini can show the other

members of the Houdini Club. But there is a trickster at the grocery store, someone who was stealing money from women's handbags. Houdini Foster, using all of his magic prowess and with the help of his cousin Janet, solves the mystery of the missing money.

Pinky and Rex and the Double Dad Weekend by James Howe
Illustrated by Melissa Sweet   Atheneum, 1995

Pinky and Rex are best friends. They can't wait to go camping and share the great outdoors with their dads. But rain comes and Pinky and Rex end up in the great indoors instead. They soon resolve their disappointment by pitching their tent in the motel room and visiting the local sights together. All agree that the great indoors is just as appealing.

The Secret Knowledge of Grown-Ups revealed and illustrated
by David Wisniewski   Lothrop, Lee & Shepard, 1998

The real reasons why adults tell children to do things such as "comb your hair" (not to keep it neat, but so it will not go back into the little holes in your head) and "don't jump on your bed" (not so you won't get hurt, but so you don't wake up the woolly creatures who live in your mattress) are unveiled with humor in this book.

Solo Girl by Andrea Pinkney
Illustrated by Nneka Bennett   Hyperion, 1997

Math comes easy to young Cass but, for the life of her, she can't learn to jump double Dutch on the school playground. She practices and practices jumping rope by herself, and steadily improves with the help of her two brothers who write some special rhymes for her. But when it comes to double Dutch, she just can't do it—until the day she figures out how math can help.

Swamp Angel by Anne Isaacs
Illustrated by Paul O. Zelinsky   Dutton, 1994

On August 1, 1815, Angelica Longrider was born in Tennessee. At first, she wasn't much different from any other child. But at age two, she built her first log cabin. And when she was full grown, she was the bravest woman around. Called Swamp Angel, she single-handedly wrestled Thundering Tarnation, the hungriest bear in Tennessee. In the end, Tennessee was too small for Swamp Angel, so she kept Thundering Tarnation's pelt as a rug and moved to Montana.

42

Do You Have Any Good Books for Third Graders?

Adventures of Captain Underpants by Dav Pilkey   Scholastic, 1997

See page 5 for a description of this book.

Bug Boy by Carol Sonenklar   Illustrated by Betsy Lewin   Henry Holt, 1997

Charlie loves bugs and knows all about them. One day an anonymous package arrives for him—inside is the Amazing Bug-a-View. Charlie thinks the Bug-a-View is just a cheap toy, until he looks at his pet spider through it and winds up with eight legs himself!

Call Me Ahnighito by Pam Conrad
Illustrated by Richard Egielski   HarperCollins, 1995

Ahnighito, a meteorite sitting for centuries on the freezing cold earth of Greenland, recounts its story. At first, snow people chip away at the meteorite for hundreds of years. Then, the meteorite is exposed to the elements even more when the earth around its sides is dug away by other men, who come back two years later to move the meteorite. But a blizzard forces the abandonment of the project until the sun warms the sky. After a turbulent voyage, the meteorite finds itself in the Brooklyn Navy Yard and sits there for seven long years. Finally moved again, Ahnighito finds home in a museum.

Donavan's Word Jar by Monalisa DeGross
Illustrated by Cheryl Hanna   HarperCollins, 1994

Third-grader Donavan loves words! When he hears or reads a word he likes, he collects it by writing it on a slip of paper and placing it in a jar. But what will Donavan do now that his word jar is filled to the brim? He asks his parents, grandma, and teacher for advice, and finally comes up with the solution on his own: words are meant to be shared.

The First Apple by Ching Yeung Russell
Illustrated by Christopher Zhong-Yuan Zang   Boyds Mills, 1994

> Nine-year-old Ying is growing up in China in the 1940s. A mischievous girl, she is forever getting herself into trouble. But Ying puts her determination and high spirits to good use when she decides to acquire an apple to give to her grandmother on her birthday, because it's something that both Ying and her grandmother have read about but never have tasted.

How to Be Cool in the Third Grade by Betsy Duffey
Illustrated by Janet Wilson   Viking, 1993

> Robbie plans to be cool now that he's in the third grade. He has to convince his mother not to kiss him at the bus stop anymore and get rid of his super-hero underwear. His first day, though, turns out to be very uncool. His mom takes his picture at the bus stop, and he trips getting on the bus and lands in a bully's lap. Robbie then has to figure out how to get around these and other obstacles to become cool.

Marvin Redpost: Why Pick on Me? by Louis Sachar
Illustrated by Barbara Sullivan   Random, 1993

> A small incident during recess threatens to turn nine-year-old Marvin into the outcast of his third-grade class. He is unfairly accused of being a nose-picker, and no one will stand in Marvin's defense. So Marvin conducts a survey to ask his classmates, and even his teacher and principal, if they have ever picked their noses. Does everyone answer honestly?

Meet Addy: An American Girl by Connie Porter
Illustrated by Melodye Rosales   Pleasant, 1993

> It's 1864 and Addy, a nine-year-old slave, lives with her family on a plantation in North Carolina. Addy has to work in the fields, picking fat green worms off cotton. Then she is responsible for taking water to the field hands, and, finally, taking food to her master. When Addy overhears her master talk about selling her father and brother, Addy runs to warn them. But she is too late. Now, leaving her little sister behind, Addy and her mother must escape alone. Traveling only by night, Addy and her mother heroically find their way to the railroad tracks and to the little white house with red shutters. There, a kindly old lady hides them in her wagon and takes them to the coast so they can catch a ship to Philadelphia and to freedom.

Nim and the War Effort by Milly Lee
Illustrated by Yangsook Choi   Frances Foster, 1997

See page 86 for a description of this book.

See You Around, Sam! by Lois Lowry
Illustrated by Diane DeGroat   Houghton Mifflin, 1996

Anastasia's little brother Sam loves his new plastic fangs. He especially loves hearing people scream. The problem is that his mother does not love his fangs, and forbids him to wear them in the house. Sam knows that there must be a nicer place to live where he can wear his fangs, so he decides to run away.

The Skirt by Gary Soto   Illustrated by Eric Velasquez   Delacorte, 1992

Soon after she gets off the school bus on Friday aftenoon, Miata Ramirez realizes that she left her special folklórico skirt on board. Not only is it her mother's special skirt from Mexico, she needs it for a folk dance performance on Sunday afternoon. Using all her problem-solving skills, Miata works all weekend to try to get the skirt back in time for her performance.

Three Terrible Trins by Dick King-Smith
Illustrated by Mark Teague   Crown, 1994

Poor Mrs. Gray is left alone to raise her three boys after the cat eats her husband. The three mouse brothers avenge their father's death as soon as they are old enough and able enough to concoct a plan. Then they set about bringing all the mice in Orchard House together, against established mouse society rules, for soccer games.

Tooter Pepperday by Jerry Spinelli
Illustrated by Donna Nelson   Random House, 1995

Tooter Pepperday and her family are moving from the city to a farm in the country. Tooter doesn't want to go. When the family arrives in the country, Tooter hates the smells of the farm. Even more, she hates the fact that there is no McDonald's down the street. Why, the pizza man won't even deliver pizza to the farm! Tooter is depressed, disgusted, and determined to find a way back to the city. But soon Tooter begins to change. She no longer hates everything, and eventually, she realizes that farm life is not so bad after all.

Wild Willie and King Kyle Detectives by Barbara M. Joosse
Illustrated by Sue Truesdell   Clarion, 1993

Willie and Kyle's plans for a summer detective agency are spoiled when Kyle's family moves to Cleveland, Ohio. Willie carries on though, with help from Kyle through the mail, by spying on the girl who moves into Kyle's old house. The mysterious girl next door seems to have lots of oddly dressed friends, and much to Willie's surprise, she also plays baseball!

43

Do You Have Any Good Books for Fourth Graders?

The Absolutely True Story . . . of My Visit to Yellowstone with the Terrible Rupes by Willo Davis Roberts   Atheneum, 1994

> Twelve-year-old Lewis and his twin sister Alison agree to accompany their new neighbors on a trip to Yellowstone Park. Little do they know that Mr. Rupe is a terrible driver, that the Rupe family eats nothing but junk food, and that they will be expected to take care of the Rupe's three- and four-year-old children for most of the trip. Just when it seems things cannot get worse, Lewis notices that they are being followed!

Allergic to My Family by Liza Murrow   Holiday House, 1992

> Rosie Maxwell, the second child of the five Maxwell children, feels that no one in her family is paying attention to her. She tries to do good things to get noticed, but ends up with unwelcome results. When a fire threatens their California home, Rosie's quick thinking in this crisis gains her the appreciation she has been seeking.

Boys at Work by Gary Soto   Illustrated by Robert Casilla   Delacorte, 1995

> When ten-year-old Rudy Herrera accidentally breaks a CD player belonging to tough guy, Trucha Mendoza, he knows he's in big trouble. He and his best friend Alex join forces to work a series of odd jobs to earn the money to replace the disc player before Trucha gets home from his summer vacation.

Dear Levi: Letters from the Overland Trail by Elvira Woodruff
Illustrated by Beth Peck   Knopf, 1994

> This story, told in letters, details Austin's trip west from Pennsylvania to Oregon. Having lost both his parents, Austin is traveling with a group of

families by wagon to find the land that their father had claimed for them. He writes letters home to his younger brother Levi about the group's many adventures along the way.

Gib Rides Home by Zilpha Keatley Snyder   Delacorte, 1998

Ten-year-old Gib Whittaker lives at the Lovell House Home for Orphaned and Abandoned Boys. Life at the home is hard, but he's heard stories about other boys being farmed out to worse situations. Now he learns that he is being sent to the Thorntons' Rocking M Ranch. Here Gib finds hard work from dawn to dusk but a better situation than living at Lovell House. Will the Thorntons decide to keep him?

Mayfield Crossing by Vaunda Micheaux Nelson   Putnam, 1993

See page 96 for a description of this book.

Poison Ivy and Eyebrow Wigs by Bonnie Pryor
Illustrated by Gail Owens   Morrow, 1993

Martin Elwood Snodgrass feels that he is not famous or special like the rest of his family. He is in the fourth grade this year and is determined to somehow join the in-crowd of cool boys. But Martin doesn't like sports, and he's got very bushy eyebrows. Will the cool and popular kids want him for a friend?

Ramona's World by Beverly Cleary
Illustrated by Alan Tiegreen   Morrow, 1999

See page 6 for a description of this book.

A School for Pompey Walker by Michael Rosen   Illustrated by
Aminah Brenda Lynn Robinson   Harcourt, Brace, 1995

Pompey Walker tells the story of his life in a speech following the dedication of a school named after him. As a seven-year-old slave, Pompey Bibb, he was put to work in the stables. When Pompey was twelve, a horse in his care reared up and hurled a white man, Jeremiah Walker, across a fence. For that, Charles Bibb had Pompey beaten, but Jeremiah Walker remained kind to Pompey. Eventually Pompey was sold to Jeremiah Walker, the son-in-law of Charles Bibb. During his time with Jeremiah Walker, whose name he took, Pompey maintained a dream of building a school for former slaves. After many experiences, they did build a school named Sweet Freedom.

Star Hatchling by Margaret Bechard   Puffin, 1997

See page 30 for a description of this book.

Suitcase by Mildred Pitts Walter   Illustrated by
Teresa Flavin   Lothrop, Lee & Shepard, 1999

Everyone at school calls Xander "Suitcase," a mean-spirited joke about the size of his shoes. He's so much taller than other kids his age that everyone expects him to be a natural at basketball, but he's no good at the sport at all. In fact, he's much more interested in art, and he even creates an award-winning poster at school. When a leader at the neighborhood center recognizes that Xander has excellent hand-eye coordination, he suggests that he give pitching a try. Soon Xander has a new talent, as well as a new hero who was also stuck with a nickname: the great pitcher Satchel Paige.

Trolls by Polly Horvath   Farrar, Straus, & Giroux, 1999

When Melissa, Amanda, and Pee Wee's parents go to Paris for a week, their father's sister, Aunt Sally, comes to baby-sit. The eccentric aunt, whom the children know only from Christmas cards, comes with stories from her childhood on Vancouver Island in British Columbia. These are not just any old stories; they contain characters like a dog named Mrs. Gunderson, Great-uncle Louis, who is an avid vegetable eater, and mysterious trolls. Besides telling stories Aunt Sally makes Pee Wee a tree house and sews everyone a Halloween costume. And, nobody else could eat a green bean like Aunt Sally.

Yang the Youngest and His Terrible Ear by Lensey Namioka
Illustrated by Kees de Kiefte   Little, Brown, 1992

Everyone in the Yang family is musically talented except Fourth Brother, Yingtao. Now that they have moved to the United States, Yingtao's father wants to make a good impression so that he will get more music students. Will Yingtao be able to learn his music in time for the recital? How can he tell his father that he'd really rather be playing baseball?

Your Mother Was a Neanderthal by Jon Scieszka
Illustrated by Lane Smith   Viking, 1993

See page 38 for a description of this book.

44

Do You Have Any Good Books for Fifth Graders?

Birchbark House by Louise Erdrich   Hyperion, 1999

In 1847, seven-year-old Omakayas lives with her Ojibwa family on an island in Lake Superior her people call Island of the Golden Breasted Woodpecker. She lives with her mother, her father, her grandmother, her beautiful older sister Angeline, her annoying brother Little Pinch, and her baby brother Neewo. In the spring, Omakayas and her family build a birch house, a summerhouse, where they will tan hides, fish, and plant their crops. Life is good in summer and into the fall. Then the harshness of winter brings a white man's disease—smallpox. Soon, sickness and death overtake Omakayas' family and other people in the village. But Omakayas and her grandmother are spared from the disease. As she cares for her family, baby Neewo dies. Only the truth sets Omakayas free of the sadness inside her.

The Boggart by Susan Cooper   Maxwell Macmillan, 1993

Emily and Jess cannot believe their family has inherited a castle in Scotland. Once there, they are surprised to find that the castle also comes with its very own Boggart, a mischievous ghost who plays tricks on the castle's residents. When a desk is shipped from the castle to their home back in Canada, Emily and Jess discover that the Boggart is inside. How can they explain all the strange things that are happening now that the Boggart lives with them? And can they possibly figure out a way to return a homesick Boggart to the castle in Scotland?

Frindle by Andrew Clements   Illustrated by
Brian Selznick   Simon & Schuster, 1996

See page 5 for a description of this book.

Hester Bidgood: Investigatrix of Evill Deedes by E. W. Hildick
Macmillan, 1994

A young girl in 1692 New England must solve the mystery of an abused cat before an innocent woman is accused of witchcraft. When the towns-people emerge from the meeting house to find Goody Wilson's gray kitten lying there with the mark of the cross on it, the rumors of her witchcraft begin to fly. Only Hester, with help from Rob, begins to question who could have played such a cruel prank.

Jennifer Murdley's Toad: A Magic Shop Book by Bruce Coville
Illustrated by Gary A. Lippincott   Harcourt, Brace, 1992

When Jennifer wanders into the magic shop and buys a talking toad, she has no idea of the trouble it will cause her and her friends. Bufo talks all the time and pretty soon Jennifer has to share her secret with her friend Ellen. But then rude, nosey Sharra wants to see the toad too. Much to Sharra's surprise, Bufo jumps up and kisses her right on the lips. But instead of turning Bufo into a prince, the kiss causes Sharra to turn into a toad! Now what will Jennifer do?

Jip: His Story by Katherine Paterson   Lodestar, 1996

See page 93 for a description of this book.

The Mouse of Amherst by Elizabeth Spires
Illustrated by Claire A. Nivola   Farrar, Straus, & Giroux, 1999

See page 103 for a description of this book.

Off and Running by Gary Soto
Illustrated by Eric Velasquez   Delacorte, 1995

Here characters from earlier Soto novels come together in a race for fifth-grade class president. Serious Miata Ramirez from *The Skirt* (Delacorte, 1992) campaigns against class clown Rudy Herrera from *The Pool Party* (Delacorte, 1993). While Miata's platform focuses on a school beautification project, Rudy's running for extended recess and the addition of ice cream to school lunches. Comic encounters between the two candidates move the story along in a series of humorous episodes.

Ribbons by Laurence Yep   Putnam, 1996

Eleven-year-old Robin wants to be a dancer when she grows up, so she bitterly resents her family's decision to suspend her lessons so they can afford to bring their grandmother from Hong Kong to San Francisco. To make matters worse, Grandma is a crotchety woman who prefers Robin's younger brother to her. But Robin eventually comes to appreciate her when she hears the story behind Grandma's mangled feet and learns about the tradition of foot binding.

The Warm Place by Nancy Farmer   Orchard, 1995

See page 104 for a description of this book.

The Watsons Go to Birmingham—1963 by Christopher Paul Curtis Delacorte, 1995

See page 98 for a description of this book.

Yolonda's Genius by Carol Fenner   Margaret K. McElderry, 1995

See page 83 for a description of this book.

INDEX

Sharon Deeds is Head of Youth and Media Services at the Cobb County Public Library System in Marietta, Georgia, where she has worked for over ten years. She received her MLS from Florida State University in Tallahassee, Florida.

Catherine Chastain is the media specialist at Westside Middle School in Winder, Georgia. She holds an MLS from Louisiana State University and worked for eight years as a children's librarian and youth services coordinator for the Clayton County Library System in Jonesboro, Georgia.